THIS BOOK BELONGS TO

Books have the power to change lives.

SureShot Books Publishing LLC is part of the SureShot 2k family
of companies that was founded in 1990 to help inmates & their
families by making it possible to improve their lives with the
Power of Reading.

Here at SureShot Books, we fervently believe that the fact that
you have made a mistake does and should not mean that your life
is ruined forever.

We believe that everyone deserves a second chance.

Contact Us with any questions or concerns:
SureShot Books Publishing LLC
P.O. Box 924, Nyack, New York 10960
845.675.7505
Email Us:
info@sureshotbooks.com

TABLE OF CONTENT

HOW TO PLAY SUDOKU

SuDoku is a grid-based puzzle. It's fun to solve them, and you don't need to be a math genius to do it!

This puzzle book has 9x9 grid (81 squares) puzzles. These grids are structured in rows, columns. Also, the grid consists of nine 3x3 sub-grids called Boxes. All rows, columns, and boxes must be filled in with numbers from 1-9. There is, however, a catch. Each number can only appear once in each row, column, and box.

In order to begin a Sudoku puzzle, simply scan the rows and columns within each triple-box region, eliminating numbers or squares and finding situations where only one number fits.

However, challenging Sudoku puzzles might require a deeper mental analysis.

The following are some techniques for solving puzzles:

1. One or two-dimensional scanning

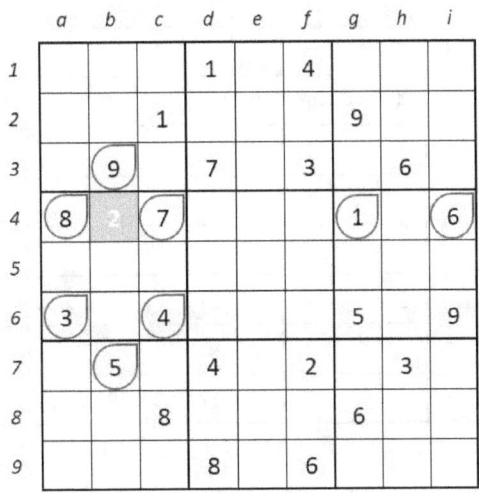

This example shows where 1 can be placed in Box-3. Row-1 and Row-2 contain 1s, leaving two empty squares in Box-3's bottom. Square g4 also contains a 1, so Column g cannot contain another 1. Therefore, Square i3 is the only place left for 1.

2. Searching and identifying single candidates

	a	b	c	d	e	f	g	h	i
1				1		4			
2			1				9		
3		9		7		3		6	
4	8	2	7				1		6
5									
6	3		4				5		9
7		5		4		2		3	
8			8				6		
9				8		6			

When you scan easy puzzles carefully, you will often find that 8 unique digits have already been used in the relevant row, column, or box.

For the Square b4: we can see that 3, 4, 7, and 8 are already used in the same box -4, 1 and 6 are already used in the same row, and 5 and 9 are already used in the same column. As a result of eliminating all the above numbers, only 2 remains as a candidate for Square b4.

3. Eliminating Numbers from Boxes, Columns and Rows

	a	b	c	d	e	f	g	h	i
1			9	2		3	8		
2			1			9			
3	4		8	6		5	1		3
4	1		2				9		4
5									
6	8		3				5		2
7	9		6	5	1?	2	3		7
8			1						
9			5	4	1?	8	6		

Sometimes the elimination of numbers can become a little complex and tricky.

As shown in this example, Square c8 contains 1, which means that Square e7 or Square e9 must also contain 1. In any case, the 1 in box-8 is in column-e. Therefore, the 1 can't be in Box-2's center column. The only square in Box 2 that can hold 1 is Square d2.

4. Using naked pairs in a box to eliminate squares

	a	b	c	d	e	f	g	h	i
1	4			8		9	1		
2			7					9	
3	9	5			2				7
4	1				9				3
5	3	9	2	4			7	8	
6	6				3				9
7	7	2	4 9		8			6	
8		1	4 9				2		
9		6	3	1		2			4

As shown in this example, square c7 and square c8 are the only places where 4 and 9 can be found. We don't know which square will have the specific number. We have, however, narrowed it down to two numbers.

Additionally, Square a6 prevents 6 from appearing in the left column of Box 7.

This means that the 6 can only be placed in Square b9. When the same pair can be placed in only two boxes, they are called Disjoint Subsets. When Disjoint Subsets are easily visible, they are called Naked Pairs. This technique can be applied to boxes as well as rows and columns.

Harmony Squares: LGBT Sudoku Series

Puzzle # 1 Easy

4			8				9	7
	8		6			4		
	3		4	2		5		
		2	5	8	3	6		
6		8	2					
	7	4	1	6	9			
	9	5	3					2
				4	8	7		5
	4			5	2	9	6	1

Puzzle # 2 Easy

4		9	2			7		5
7					1	4		6
		1	4			8	9	
9		5	6	3		1		
2								9
				4		6	5	7
	4					9	3	1
	9	7	1			5		8
8	1	6		5				4

Puzzle # 3 Easy

*	5	1			3		7
9					2	4	1
	7	9		5	6		
5	6		2	1	8		9	3
1	9		3	7		2	
			2	1			
8	3	9	5	6		1	7	2
		7		9			5

Puzzle # 4 Easy

		5		9	3			
9	4	1	2		7			
3	6	8			5			9
7	3						8	2
			6	4		8		5
8	5			7		9	1	4
			3		7	4	2	
			9	3				7
5			7	6				8

Puzzle # 5 Easy

4		8	5			1		7
			8	4			5	
6	5		9	7	1			
5				9	3			2
			3	4	7			
1	3		2					9
3		9	4	8		2	1	
		5	6	9			3	8
8	6							

Puzzle # 6 Easy

5	2			7		3		8
9		4		3	5	2		6
			8		2			
7						6		2
	1	9		2	6	7		
		7			8	1	9	3
		1				5	6	
	3		5		9	4		
	4	5			7		3	

Puzzle # 7 Easy

		3		1				9
4				7			1	3
1	5		9		8	6		
9		5	3	8		2		
6		8	4	9	2		3	
		1		6	7		9	
					3		8	
8	6	4			9		5	
3		9	8				4	

Puzzle # 8 Easy

3		5				8	4	
7			3			5		
	4		1					
8	7		9	5	2	1	3	6
2		6	4		7		5	
			8		3	2	7	4
	5							9
	9	5		1		7		
6	2				8	4		5

Puzzle # 9 Easy

	3					8	4	
		2	7			3	6	5
7					8		1	
6	2						5	3
				2		1	7	
9	7					4		
	1	6			5	7	3	4
	4	7		6	3	5		8
5	9		4			6		

Puzzle # 10 Easy

	9	5	3		1	6		
3			7	5		8	9	
8		7			9	3		
1	3						8	6
		8				2		
6	7	9			2		1	5
	8							
	2	1	6		7			
		3	5	9	8	1	2	

Puzzle # 11 Easy

				2	4			1
5			1			3	7	
						9		
1			4			7	8	
	4		7	2	5	9	1	6
		7		9		3	4	2
2				8	9		7	4
	8	6	2			3	1	5
9				5	4			

Puzzle # 12 Easy

3	4	5	7	9	8	6	1	
							4	5
	6			2		3		9
	7		9	5		2		4
5				6		9	3	7
					7		5	8
9		2	1					
	6			7			9	
	1			4		5		3

Puzzle # 13 Easy

		1	4		5			
				5	2			
9	7		2		6	4		1
		8				3		
	5		6	2		9		
6			3			1		5
	9	7			2		1	3
8			9	6	1	5	2	
		6				8	9	4

Puzzle # 14 Easy

1								6
6		8	5	9		2		
					7	9	8	3
	2			7		4	6	
3					2	7		9
7		6		1		3		8
4	2	9	8					7
	6	3		2		8		4
	7					6	5	2

Puzzle # 15 Easy

1	4	2		8	7	9		
			6		9		7	
9			3		2		1	
5			4	2		3		1
	3			9		4	2	
2			7	3	1	6	8	5
	5		1	6		8		
		3		7				
4			2					

Puzzle # 16 Easy

	7			5			1	8
	3							7
			7		1	9		
9	1		5	4	8	3		2
3				9				
	4	8	2		3		9	
	9	3	8	6		1	5	4
	8			1		2		6
	6		4	3				9

Puzzle # 17 Easy

1	3		4		7			
2	7	8		3				
		4	8					
	4					1		8
8		2				4	7	
			2	4	8	3	5	6
	6	1			4			
	8	3	9	6		2		7
9	2			8	3			5

Puzzle # 18 Easy

1	5		7		9			
		6	1	2			8	
4				5	3	7		6
		4	8	7	2	5	1	
7		5					4	
							6	
5		9	2	7		6		8
			9	6	4	7		
	7		4	8			9	2

Puzzle # 19 Easy

			3		7	5		
6				4			3	2
	9		5	8	2			6
2		7	1		9			
1				5	2			4
3	5			8			9	1
	3	6		7	1	9	2	
			8		3			
7			2		3			

Puzzle # 20 Easy

2		5			7		9	
	7		5		9	6	2	
6	3	9			1	5	7	4
	9			6	4			2
	6	8						5
	2	3				7		9
9	1		2	5			3	7
				9				8
7		2				9		6

Harmony Squares: LGBT Sudoku Series

Puzzle # 21 Easy

		6				4	1	3
7	4			3	9			5
3	5		1			9	8	7
		4	2					9
2		5					6	
			9		6	2		
4	6			9	2		5	1
9	3				8			6
5				6		3	9	

Puzzle # 22 Easy

		6				9		
	8		6		9		4	7
5			8	2			6	3
6	4		7	9			3	5
7	3					4		
	5				1		7	
4		3	9			7		
9		7		8	5	3	1	4
8	1					6		

Puzzle # 23 Easy

	7			4			5	3
4		3		5		1	7	
1	2		8	3	7			4
	4	7		9				
	8	1			4		6	7
3				7	8			
	1		2	8			3	
			4					1
5	9			1		4	8	

Puzzle # 24 Easy

			6					
1			8	4		2		
		7		1	9			
2		9				6		
	7	8	2		1		5	3
5			6	4	9	7		
6			9	7	8			4
7	4	2	1	3	6		9	
9				5		4	1	

Puzzle # 25 Easy

7			8				3	4
						5	6	
5	6	4	3	2	1	9		7
				1		6	2	
		6	7			4	1	3
1			6		3		5	8
	7		1			3		
9			5				4	6
	8	3			9			

Puzzle # 26 Easy

8			3				1	7
	7		1					5
1		9		4	5	2		
			7				4	
7	5				4		8	
4	8	2		5			9	
2	4		5	6	8		7	
5	9		4		7	6		
	1		2	3			5	

Puzzle # 27 Easy

			1	4	6		5	
	3	6	7				1	
8		1		9		6	7	
			9				6	
		9	2			1		
7		2			4	5	3	9
1		3		2	7	4	8	5
	5							
	7		4	5	9	3	2	

Puzzle # 28 Easy

	7		8				5	3
3			4			1	8	
			3	1				7
7		3			4			2
8		2				6		
4	5				3			8
5		8	9		6	4	7	
6		1						
9	3		4	5	1	8	2	

Puzzle # 29 Easy

		8					5	2
	6	8			5	9	1	
5				9		4		
		9	1		2	3	8	4
8	3		5	4		1	9	6
4			3		9			
				6	5		9	
	7				4		2	1
9	4			5				

Puzzle # 30 Easy

1		9	5			8		4
				8			5	
5			4	6				7
6		5	7	4	3		8	
	7	8	9			5		3
3			8				7	9
		7	3		4			
4	5				8		3	2
8	3		1					

Puzzle # 31 Easy

			7		4			5
5	4		9	3		2		
7	8		6	2	5		9	1
						6		2
3	1	7	4	6			5	
		8	5		7		1	
		2	8		9	1		
		4						
1				4		5	8	

Puzzle # 32 Easy

		4	3	9	5	2	7	8
5					1	4		6
		7		6	4		3	5
6	4	3	9		2			1
		1	4	5		3		
			1	8		9		
	5				9			
		6		4				
7				3	8			2

11

Harmony Squares: LGBT Sudoku Series

Puzzle # 33 Easy

				1		4	8	
			4	2				7
4		3		8	5	2		
8			2	7	4		6	5
	5	4		9		7		8
7		9		8		4		
	8	2		5			1	9
		7	6	2			5	
5			8					

Puzzle # 34 Easy

	3	5	2		8		1	4
	8	9	7				5	
	4			5	9			8
	6	3	8		9		4	
	9	4		1		8	6	7
			5			3	9	1
3				2			8	
			5	8		2		
4	2							5

Puzzle # 35 Easy

		9	3	4			5	2
7	4		9		2		3	6
	8	2		5		4	9	
9			8	2				
		7	1	3			4	
	3		7	6	5			9
	7				3	5		
	6							
	9		4	7		3		8

Puzzle # 36 Easy

	4	5		2	3			
7		9			1	2		6
1						4		
	9	3				7	8	5
4	7	8		5				1
5	6		7			3	2	4
8				3				2
				6	9		4	
		4	5				6	3

Puzzle # 37 Easy

		1	6	4	7			
	7	5	1		9	3		
		3		7				1
	4	6		2				5
9	5	2		4			8	
			7		5	2	4	
6	2	9			7	8	1	
5	3				8			
		7				5		4

Puzzle # 38 Easy

8		4	7		9		2	
		2	1	4			9	
9			6	2		4	7	8
2	5			6			1	
			3		1			
6	1	3		5	2			
3								2
	9			7		8	3	
4				1		7	6	9

Puzzle # 39 Easy

3			7					8
8			6	4		7		
5	7			2	8	3		
6	4		9					5
9	5	2	4				1	
			5	7	9	4		
7						5		4
	3	5		1				
2	9	6		7		1	8	

Puzzle # 40 Easy

	4			8			5	6
	1	2		6				9
	6	8	1	9		3	4	2
1		5	8	2	9			
8	2	3	9		4		1	5
	9		1					
4		7				9		
					1			7
	3				7	4		8

Puzzle # 41 Easy

2	5		8	4	3	7	9	
		4	5		6	2		3
3		7					5	4
7	9				2			5
6		8	1		4			2
			3			8	1	
	2	3	4			5		9
				2		3	4	
			3				2	

Puzzle # 42 Easy

2			6	1	9			
		1		3				
	9	3	5		2			
					3		5	1
			1	6		9	3	
3	1	6				4	2	8
	3			5	8			
8		7		2	1		6	9
1	2		7		6			4

Puzzle # 43 Easy

4		8			3			
7	5	3		2				6
9			8	7			2	
		5			8			
1	4		7		6	2		8
8		7					4	
6		1				4	7	
3				9	7		1	
5			6	1			8	3

Puzzle # 44 Easy

8		3						1
6	2	9	8	4	1			
	7	1				8	4	
					9	4	8	7
			7	1		3		9
				8			1	
2			9		8	5		4
7		4		5	6		9	8
			1				3	6

Puzzle # 45 Easy

1	2	5			3	7		9
		8		9	7			1
4	9				6	8		2
5		9				3		
	1	6	4	3	2			8
		2			9			6
	6		9					
2				8	4	9		
9	7		3	2			8	

Puzzle # 46 Easy

5	8		6	9				
	3			5		2	9	
	7		1	3	5			8
7						1		
	5	6	4		1		8	9
9	1		6					
	2			4		9		1
3	9	7			8	4		
1	6					3		

Puzzle # 47 Easy

	1		7	6	4	9	2	
			3	8	2			
	2						3	6
1	5		4	9	6	7		
	8	6	5					3
			1			9		
		4	8	5	1	3		
	3	8		4			7	1
		1	2		3			

Puzzle # 48 Easy

	6	9	3		8		1	5
		4	2		9	8	6	
2	8							
	3	8			4	7		1
			8		3		4	
4	2		9	1	7			
	4			9		5		6
6	1				5	9		
			3	6				7

Puzzle # 49 Easy

4	2	9				5	1	
	1	3		9			7	
	6		3					9
		1	8	7		2		
6	8	4	1		2	9		
	5	7			6		8	
							4	
1	4			6		7	9	
	7		4			3	5	6

Puzzle # 50 Easy

3	4		6	7				
	5			2	9	3		8
					5	6		
		2	4			9	1	7
7			9	1	6			5
		9	8		7	4	3	6
4					1			3
		7		6			8	4
8	2						6	

Puzzle # 51 Medium

		6	2			4		
	9				2			1
				9			5	6
3		9		6			7	2
			1	5	3	4	9	
8				4			1	5
					6			
4		2	6					

Puzzle # 52 Medium

3		4			8		7	
	5							
	9		1	2		4		6
2	6			1				
5		8	3		6			
1	4	3			6			
	3				1			7
4				5			9	
			9			3		8

Puzzle # 53 Medium

	3		4				2	5
9	2		5		3	8		
	4	1			2		7	
4	6	8		3	5	2		
	1		2	4	6	5	8	
							3	
	8	5				6		
		4	3	5	8			
1				6	4			8

Puzzle # 54 Medium

		4				8	5	
4	6					2		7
		8	5	7		6	4	1
		1			8	4		
							3	2
			2	7		5	6	
	2					3		4
	1				6	7		
		7		8	4			

Puzzle # 55 Medium

	5		2			3		
	6			4	1			5
			6			7		
	8		9		3	2	4	6
		2					8	
6		4					1	
	2		4	9		6		1
4	1		3		2	7		
9	7				1			8

Puzzle # 56 Medium

2			1			3	8	
		8	6	7			5	
		6	8	2			9	
			3					9
5	3			1	7			
					9		3	
7					8	9	6	
	8	5		6		1		
6		3			1	2		

Puzzle # 57 Medium

					3			
		1			5	8	6	
	6		3			4	9	5
9	1				8	6		
8	2	3				1	4	
	5							8
1			7		6		2	
6	4			5		7		
3	7	5	1	2			8	

Puzzle # 58 Medium

	3	2					9	6
9	5							
		4			1			7
		6		1				3
4		5		9				
				6			7	4
	2	7				4		
6		9	4	3				
1	4	3			7	2	6	

Puzzle # 59 Medium

7	5	9		8			2	
				4			5	
3			5		2		7	
		2			3	6		7
		5	6					4
		7						
4	7		9					1
	6		1					3
	9					4		

Puzzle # 60 Medium

			1	8		4		
		4	9		5			
	1				7			5
3			8	9			7	
7	5							1
					1			
		4	7	6		9	8	
6	4		5	2		1		

Puzzle # 61 Medium

	7	5				1		
4				7			2	
2	6		1					
3	1	4				6		5
	2	8		1	3	7		
7								
			2	4			7	
	5	6			9			4

Puzzle # 62 Medium

	5	3	1			9		6
8		7	2					5
	2				9			
	4		6				9	
3		8		2	5	7		
	1							
2		4		9			3	
	3	1	4			5		
	8			1			6	

Puzzle # 63 Medium

	3	6	1					
2		8	9					7
		7		8		5	6	
	5				9	3		
	2		8					
	8	1		2		7	9	
	5		2			4	6	
1			7					
	6			9	8			1

Puzzle # 64 Medium

2				7	5			
	7	8				4		5
		1		4	3	7	8	
			7		1		5	3
	9		3					
				6		9	7	8
			4	3		5	1	
7							4	
5		6			9	8		

Puzzle # 65 Medium

						4	1	7
3			4	1				
	7				6		3	
		6			3			
7	9	3	1			6		4
	4	2		7				
	3	9				5	6	1
6	5	4	8					
	1		9	6	5	8	4	3

Puzzle # 66 Medium

8	6		5			1		2
3		1	6	8			4	5
	5			4	3		8	
			8	6		2		4
				4			7	
	7		3	2		1		6
2	3	9	7		6			
1	4	5					6	7

Puzzle # 67 Medium

	6	8	7				3	2
9					5			
	2		6			1		9
	8	9	3	4				
7	5				8		1	
						9	4	
5			8			7		
2	1		4		6			5
				7		2		

Puzzle # 68 Medium

	7			8		1		
			7				8	3
5	8	1	4			7		
	3	8			6		5	
		2				9	7	
		6		2		3		
	1	5	2				3	
8	6							4
		3			8			

Puzzle # 69 Medium

```
. . 8 | . 9 . | 6 . 3
. 1 . | . 6 . | 5 8 .
. . . | 8 3 . | . 1 .
------+-------+------
6 . 5 | 7 . 4 | 1 . 9
. 8 . | 9 . 3 | 2 . .
. . . | . . . | . . .
------+-------+------
2 . 6 | . . 4 | . . .
8 . 1 | . . . | . 2 .
. 5 9 | . . 8 | . 6 .
```

Puzzle # 70 Medium

```
. . . | . 1 . | . . .
. 3 . | 8 9 . | . . 7
. 7 5 | . . . | . 1 .
------+-------+------
. . . | 4 7 6 | 9 . 8
. . . | . . . | . . .
. 6 4 | 5 2 . | 1 . .
------+-------+------
. . 1 | . . 7 | . 5 .
. . . | 1 8 . | 4 . .
4 . . | 9 . 5 | . . .
```

Puzzle # 71 Medium

```
6 . 3 | . . . | . 9 .
. 1 2 | . 9 . | . . .
. . . | . 3 . | 7 . .
------+-------+------
. 3 5 | 7 4 2 | 6 . .
8 7 . | . . . | 5 . 4
. . 1 | . 6 . | 9 . .
------+-------+------
1 2 4 | . . . | . . .
. . . | 7 . . | . . 1
. . . | 1 . . | 6 9 .
```

Puzzle # 72 Medium

```
9 . . | 8 5 6 | . . .
6 . . | 3 . . | . . .
. 4 2 | 7 . . | 1 . .
------+-------+------
. . . | . 7 . | 3 9 .
4 . . | 3 . . | . 7 .
. 5 . | 9 4 . | . . .
------+-------+------
. . 1 | 4 2 . | . . .
. . . | 3 1 . | 9 8 .
. . . | 2 8 . | 4 . .
```

Puzzle # 73 Medium

6	5					4		
		8	6		2	7		
	7				9			1
5	8	2		9			1	
7		9					8	
4			2	5	9			7
			1	4				6
9	6		3			1		
						5	9	8

Puzzle # 74 Medium

1		6	7	9			5	2
	5		1			4		
	3							
4	9							1
8	1					3		9
3	6		9					5
						7		
	8	4						6
	7	1	5		2	9		

Puzzle # 75 Medium

	9	8		6	7	5		
5					2			
6			5	7	9			8
8			1				3	7
	2	3						1
				7	9		5	
4	1			5				
7				4			9	2

Puzzle # 76 Medium

6	5		4	9				
		9	1	2		6		
		2	5		3		9	
	7	5						3
	8	1		4			6	
	9				2			1
	6				1	8		5
		8		3	6	1		
	8					9	2	

Harmony Squares: LGBT Sudoku Series

Puzzle # 77 Medium

1		3	6			5		
8					4			
6	4							
	6	8	9			1		
9			1					7
	3		2			6		
	9				1		4	2
				3			8	
	8	2				7	5	

Puzzle # 78 Medium

9	2					4		6
7						2		
3	4			9		1		
			1		8		4	
	1	2			7			
			6	4	3			
2	3	8	6					9
	9			1		6		
			7					

Puzzle # 79 Medium

	1		6		5	7		
9			3		7	5		
5		6						9
3			2	5		9		4
8								7
		5				1	3	
	5		4		2		7	
	2			6				
7	3	4					1	2

Puzzle # 80 Medium

7	5							
8			7					1
4			8		3		9	6
	8	7		4			6	
	6		9					3
				1	8	5		
9	1			7		6	3	5
	3		9	6			7	8
6		8				1		

Puzzle # 81 Medium

9		4	2	5				8
		8		3				
2						9	7	1
					5			
4		5		1		7	2	
		9	8		7			
						1	4	
	9				3			2
8								9

Puzzle # 82 Medium

7	4		5				6	
		5	6	9		3		
			4		1	8		
				9	6			
1				7				3
	5	3	8		6			9
	2	4	7			9		
		8		4			3	6
			8		5			

Puzzle # 83 Medium

	4			7		2		
2	7					5	8	
		8		9				
3				8				
			7	5		1		8
	5		1				7	3
		2						
	3	1	5					2
6			9	2		4		

Puzzle # 84 Medium

						9		
5				9		3	4	8
		2			4	7		5
6	9	4	1	2				7
	2			6	5			1
3	5		4			6		
4							7	
2	8				7	5		
1	7	9				2		3

Harmony Squares: LGBT Sudoku Series

Puzzle # 85 Medium

	6				4		1	8
4				7	6			
	8		2				7	6
5	4				1	6	3	
8					9			
	2	1		6				
3		2	1	5	8			
		8	6				5	3
			3					7

Puzzle # 86 Medium

				2			9	
6		9				3		8
3					8			5
	3		6				1	4
							3	
5				2		3	7	
					9	4		
1	9		8		6			
	4	8	1					6

Puzzle # 87 Medium

	1		7		8		5	
	6		5		2		7	
		5	4	3				2
6			3					
	3		6					
			8	4	3			1
		2	4				3	7
	7	6	5					8
		4		7	5	1		

Puzzle # 88 Medium

4	7				6	2	9	
			9	2				8
9			8	4	7			3
3	6				1			
						8	7	9
5			1		9		3	
	4	1		8			2	
			7		1		6	
	9		2			3		

Puzzle # 89 Medium

7		5			3	9		
9				4		5		
	4		6		9		2	
1		3		8	2		9	5
			9		6			4
			7	3				
			5		4			
8	9							
				9		7	3	1

Puzzle # 90 Medium

		8	5	7			1	
							9	4
4	3		8		9			
	4	6	1	2				5
		7				2		
	8			5		7		
	5		9					
	7		6		8		3	2
	6		2			1		9

Puzzle # 91 Medium

7		2					1	
	1		8			9		
		4			7	5		
	4		7	8		2		
				9				
8		3			1		5	6
			6		3			5
			9	2		3	7	
3			5	7	8			

Puzzle # 92 Medium

		3	6	1		9	7	
				4				
	1	2				5		
7			4	2				6
			5	7		2		9
	5		3			8	4	7
	2		1				8	
	6							
5			2		6	4		

Puzzle # 93 Medium

		2	8					1
	6			3				8
	9						3	6
	7	4		1	9		2	
		1	7			5		9
				2				
		7			2			
5	2		1			7		
		9				3		

Puzzle # 94 Medium

	4	3	5					9
	2		9	7	4			
	8	4		1				2
		7	1			2		5
	1							3
3							1	
	7				9	5	4	
		9	8				2	1
	3				4	8	9	

Puzzle # 95 Medium

5			7	8	4		2	
			9	1		7	5	
		7	6				1	4
	2			9	7	3	6	
3	1			5				
						4		
6								
	5			4			1	6
1				8			3	

Puzzle # 96 Medium

2	6			7	5	9	3	
	1	3				8		
7			4					
	7			9	4			3
8					3			9
	3	1	8				6	
3						5	7	4
	8	9						
			3			2		

Puzzle # 97 Medium

					1	3		
1			7	5		9		8
			8	3		2		5
9	8	6				1	5	
3	7	4		1	5			
5	2			8	4	7		
	9	7		4	3	5		2
4				2		9	3	

Puzzle # 98 Medium

			1	3	8			6
6				7		1		9
				8				4
	4					7	8	
	7	5	1					
3		1		9				
	3				6	9	5	8
	4							
7				3		6		

Puzzle # 99 Medium

8		7						
1	3			4	7			
	9			5				2
	7	4				1	9	
3	5		9					
9	1	2	3		4			5
	8	9				7		
	4			1		2		
				9	5			4

Puzzle # 100 Medium

	8		6			7	3	5
	3		2					
	5			3	8			9
	2						7	
		9		1			4	
		1		7			5	2
						5		
		2		4		3		
4		5			9	8		

Puzzle # 101 Medium

9		4			2	5		
	7					2		
		3		6			1	8
8					1		6	
7			4	5	6			
4		1		8				
3			5	7				
		7	3			8		
5					8			9

Puzzle # 102 Medium

1			7	5	4	8	3	
		8		6		7		4
7								6
2			1		5	9	4	
	4			9				
		3				5	2	
		1	6					
	7	2	5	3				
						2		5

Puzzle # 103 Medium

	3	1	9		5	7	6	
5	6			7			3	
9		7		1	3		4	
6							2	
	4	5		2		1		9
	1	3				6		4
1		2	8	5	4			
			7	6	9	2	1	

Puzzle # 104 Medium

							2	
	4			1		5	7	
2						8	3	4
			9	2	7	3		
			4					
	7			8			5	
1		9	6	4	2	7		
6	5					1	9	
		4	3			5		6

Harmony Squares: LGBT Sudoku Series

Puzzle # 105 Medium

		8			9			
9	5		1			7		3
6	1		8	5	3		4	
	2		6	1		3		
7					8		5	
						6	9	2
		1	5	6		8		
			9				3	
	7		3				6	5

Puzzle # 106 Medium

8		1	3	9	7			2
	7			6	8			4
9	6						8	7
		5				7		
7		9		4	6			
	3	4		7		8	6	
		7	6			3		
		6	7			9		1
		8	9		5			

Puzzle # 107 Medium

		7				9		
	3					7		5
	9			1			4	2
2				7				6
6			3			4	2	7
	7	9		6				
	4		5			7	9	
9					1	5		
8	6					1		

Puzzle # 108 Medium

	5					7	9	6
			5		4			
3		1						
8	4			9	7	1	5	
	9	6						
2		5				3		
	3				5			1
9				1	6			5
5		2	3				8	

Puzzle # 109 Medium

			2					
			5	6				
	8						2	1
1	5			4				9
4		6			1			3
	3	9	6	5			4	7
	4				9	3		
5			7			6		
7		1						

Puzzle # 110 Medium

3		9		1		7		
6		8					5	
		2	4				3	
4			5		6	2		
2				4	3			7
	7	6		2	1			
		7	3				6	9
9			7	5				3
					9	4		2

Puzzle # 111 Medium

9	2	7	3					
6							3	2
		3			9			
	9	8	2	3		7		
7	5	2		4		8		
		6	8					
		9		5	3		7	
8		1				6		
		5		8				9

Puzzle # 112 Medium

1							4	
	5				2	7	6	
7		6	8				1	
6				8				5
4	7	3						
	1			3		2	7	
	8	1	6	4			2	
9			2	7		6	5	1
				5				4

Puzzle # 113 Medium

				1		8		
7	8					3		
				8		1	4	7
	5	6				4	7	2
				5			3	
	4	8	7				5	1
	3					5	9	
1			5				2	
	4		2		8		1	

Puzzle # 114 Medium

	8	3					4	6
6			7			2		
	2	7	1		4		8	
		1	8	5				
3	5							4
2	7				9	5		8
		4	2		8			7
	1		3			8		
	3	2		1			6	

Puzzle # 115 Medium

2		4	1		9			5
3				6				9
5							2	
		1	8	3		2		
	5	2			1		9	
6		8					4	
	4						1	
		3	7		8	5		
8					4	9		2

Puzzle # 116 Medium

	7		6			9	1	
3	1					6	8	
	8					4		
				4				
6				3		8	9	5
	3		7				6	
	9		3		1			
		1		7	5			
				4			7	8

Puzzle # 117 Medium

7	2				1			
		8					2	5
9	4		2		5	6		
3			9					4
	5	7		1	3			
	9	4		5		1		8
	7	9		3			8	
	8		5					7
		1			4	5		9

Puzzle # 118 Medium

							7	
	2			9		3	5	
3					7	6	8	9
1	7	5				8	2	
2		6		5			3	
9								5
		2		3	4	1		
8		3	9				4	
4	9	7	1		2	5		

Puzzle # 119 Medium

	3			8		9	2	6
1				2		5		3
						8		
	9	3	2			4		
2	4	8	7	1				5
		1		4	3			7
8	7	5				1		9
	2						5	
	1	6			5	3		

Puzzle # 120 Medium

9			7	6			2	
	5			8				
6	1					5		4
	6	4				8	1	
			2			4		
2	8	9						7
				3			6	8
8	9			1			4	5
5			6	8	9			

Harmony Squares: LGBT Sudoku Series

Puzzle # 121 Hard

```
5 . . | 1 8 . | . . .
. 9 . | . . . | . 7 .
. . . | . . 4 | . . 9
------+-------+------
1 . . | 7 . . | 2 . .
. . . | 2 . 3 | 9 . .
. . . | . 4 . | . . .
------+-------+------
. . 3 | . . . | 6 4 .
. . 9 | . . 2 | 5 3 .
8 . 7 | . . . | . . .
```

Puzzle # 122 Hard

```
. 3 . | . . . | 5 . 6
. . 6 | . . . | . . .
8 1 9 | 6 . . | . . .
------+-------+------
3 . . | 5 2 . | . . .
. . . | 8 . . | . . .
. . . | 1 . . | 6 8 .
------+-------+------
. 8 . | . . . | 5 . 2
5 . . | 4 7 . | . . 3
. 9 . | . . . | . 1 .
```

Puzzle # 123 Hard

```
8 . . | . 5 . | . . 9
. 9 8 | . . . | . 2 .
. 2 . | . 1 . | . 8 4
------+-------+------
. . . | . 8 . | 9 . .
. . . | . . . | 8 . 7
. 3 . | 9 . . | 1 . .
------+-------+------
. 3 5 | 6 . . | . 4 .
2 . . | 5 . . | . . .
7 . 4 | . 1 . | . 5 .
```

Puzzle # 124 Hard

```
. . 5 | . . . | . 7 .
3 . . | . 2 4 | . . 6
. 6 . | 1 . . | 4 . .
------+-------+------
. . . | . . . | . . .
. 1 9 | . . 8 | 5 . 7
. 3 . | . 6 2 | 9 . .
------+-------+------
1 . . | 2 . 9 | . 5 .
. 3 8 | . 1 . | . 6 .
7 . . | . 6 8 | . 4 .
```

Puzzle # 125 Hard

	6							
4	9				3			
8		3		2				5
				9	5		2	
			6				5	
3			7	1		6		
2			1		6	3		
9								
6	4				8			2

Puzzle # 126 Hard

	8				5		2	
	4	7		6	9			8
3						6	4	
			7	3	4			
		4						6
7	3		9				5	
			8			3	6	
		8	4					
			5	9	7			

Puzzle # 127 Hard

	3							5
		1		5		2		
4			8	2		1		
	4		7		8	1		
			5				3	
	5				6	2	7	4
						7	4	1
				1				
8		7						3

Puzzle # 128 Hard

	4		8			9		6
1					2			
5			9	1	6			
		8	3	9				
	5					2		
				1			3	
2		9						
						8		5
		5	2	3				7

Puzzle # 129 Hard

```
4 . . | . . . | 5 . .
. . 1 | . 8 . | . . 4
. 2 3 | 6 . . | 1 . .
------+-------+------
8 3 . | . 7 . | . . .
. 4 2 | . . . | . 7 .
1 . . | . . 4 | . . 8
------+-------+------
. . 5 | 9 . 7 | . . .
. . . | . . 1 | 8 9 .
9 . 1 | . . . | . 3 .
```

Puzzle # 130 Hard

```
7 . . | . 4 . | . . .
. 2 . | 1 . 6 | 7 9 .
. . . | . . . | 3 6 2
------+-------+------
. . 4 | 7 3 . | . . .
6 1 . | 5 9 . | 8 . .
3 5 . | . . . | . . .
------+-------+------
. 7 . | . . 9 | 6 . 5
. . . | . . . | 9 . .
. . 1 | 6 . 5 | . 4 .
```

Puzzle # 131 Hard

```
. . . | . . . | 3 . 4
2 7 8 | . . . | . 6 .
. . . | 5 . . | . . .
------+-------+------
. . . | 6 . . | 3 . .
. 6 . | 7 . 4 | . . .
9 . . | . 3 . | . . 1
------+-------+------
. . . | . . . | 2 . 7
6 . . | 8 . 2 | 9 5 .
. . 3 | . . . | 1 . .
```

Puzzle # 132 Hard

```
. . . | . 5 . | 3 . .
8 . . | 1 . . | . . .
. . . | . 2 . | . 9 7
------+-------+------
. . . | 7 . . | 1 . .
. 8 7 | . 4 . | . . 3
2 . 4 | . 9 6 | . . .
------+-------+------
. 2 . | . . . | 4 1 .
. . 6 | . . . | 2 . .
. 4 5 | . . . | . . .
```

Puzzle # 133 Hard

9				1	5		2	
7		8						
1				4	6			
		5				3		8
	9			7				
			9			4		
				9	2	1		
		3		2	7			
								4

Puzzle # 134 Hard

	1	4	8	3				
2			7	5				
9	5						3	
5	4			9				1
			1					
		6		2	5		8	4
			5					6
	8				3	5		
	2			4				

Puzzle # 135 Hard

		9		4			7	
	5		9					4
	6					9		
				1	7			6
4						2		9
	2		5				3	7
	3	1					4	
2			1	7				
5								

Puzzle # 136 Hard

	4		7				6	
				8		3		4
	3	7						8
	7		2	1		6		
6		8		4		5		
		3						
5	2			3			8	
			4	2				
						4		9

Puzzle # 137 Hard

	4						9	5
1			5					7
				4		8	1	
		3			7	9	8	
5		7	1					
				2				1
4		6				2		
			9			7		6
7			6	5				

Puzzle # 138 Hard

	7		5					
5						8	4	
	6		4		8			2
		9	5	8		7	2	
	3		9				6	
7	5			4				
4	7							9
						2	8	6
			9					5

Puzzle # 139 Hard

3		4						7
		5		7				
	8					4	6	
4		8						2
6			7	9				4
		2	8			1		3
	7	3			6	2		
			1		7		3	5
2			3				4	

Puzzle # 140 Hard

	6							9
1		8				4	6	
5		4	9			3	8	
7	3		8		1			4
8		1		3	5		7	6
	5	6	7					1
			6	7	3			
9	8			2	4			

Puzzle # 141 Hard

3			4		7		6	
	1			3				4
	4	2				5	7	
			2			7		
		7	1	4				
1	6				8			
		1		6		9		7
		3	8	1				
5		4	3					8

Puzzle # 142 Hard

5			2	7		8		
						7		9
	9	1						
3				9				4
	8	9				5		
		5		8	4			
	3			4		6		7
	2		3			5	9	
					8			

Puzzle # 143 Hard

		5	6	9	1			
		1	2					
4				8		6	9	
	5			2	3	7		
						5	8	
	9	2						
5							2	
	8			3	9			
			1					3

Puzzle # 144 Hard

	9	8	3		1		7	5
		3	8	7		9		
		6		5	9	1	3	
6	8		1		3			
		2		8				
5	1		6		7	2		
						8	5	9
			1	2			6	4

Puzzle # 145 Hard

2				8				
	1		5		6		4	2
						1	6	7
6	5		9	4				3
7	9							
		8	2	7				
								4
		5	6		9		8	
	2				4	9		6

Puzzle # 146 Hard

	9		8			4		6
7						2	9	
			1	4	3			
9			1	4	8			
8								
	6	1						7
		2		7				4
	8					7		
	3							2

Puzzle # 147 Hard

7	2			8			6	
						5	4	
1	3						7	
	6		7	8				
	8			4	9			
			1					
			5		9	2		
4								6
		6		1				

Puzzle # 148 Hard

8				6		9		2
	3							
		2	3			7	8	6
			2	3		6		
1		6	9					8
3	9		6	8	1			
	7					6	4	
	6			1		7		
2	8							1

Puzzle # 149 Hard

8		4						2
	5							4
1	6		3			5		
		7	5	9			2	
			8					
	1	5	2			3		
2			7		3		4	
				5				
		3	9	8				

Puzzle # 150 Hard

	9			7			1	
7		6						2
2			6	1				
				6				
	9		1				5	4
	8	9		2				7
3	7							
							7	5
	2		8	5				6

Puzzle # 151 Hard

2		8	7			6		
	9		8				3	4
5								
	6			8				9
			5		6		2	
9	5				2			
			6		1			
	4	7		2		5		
							4	6

Puzzle # 152 Hard

	3	2	7				4	
5	7		3	4		2		9
4		9	1			7	5	
						9	3	4
6		5				1		8
2	1			5	9		6	
	3	6						
7	5			3	1			

Puzzle # 153 Hard

		7						
9						5		2
1			5	3		7	8	9
				1				8
4				5				
7		5			4	2		
		1		2				
		7	3			1		6
		3	4	1	7		2	

Puzzle # 154 Hard

6			1	4				
9								
	7	4						8
			4		1	5		
8						3	6	
	6			9		1		7
	9			3		8		
	3	8						1
	5							3

Puzzle # 155 Hard

	7					3		6
	4							
8		3			9			
7			6		8	4		
	9		2	7				
			5				6	3
		2			6			9
5					2			
4			9			2		

Puzzle # 156 Hard

		9	8			4	3	
8	1		7					6
	5							
			5		6		1	
		6		8		9		
	9	5			1			
						6	4	
		6		2				
7		4		1			5	

Puzzle # 157 Hard

	5	8		1			7	6
		7		3		9		2
5				8				
	9		3			2		4
		4			9		1	
8			1				2	7
9				6	3	1		
4			5			6	9	

Puzzle # 158 Hard

4	9					6		
		5			1			
				8				1
		3	6	2			1	
			7	5			2	
						9	8	
	5							
8			3			4		
3		2	1					

Puzzle # 159 Hard

2			6	3				
5	8	4						
7						2		
	4	6	7					
8				5	6			4
			3			7		
			3	7				6
	3	8	2			7	4	
		5			9	2		

Puzzle # 160 Hard

						8	7	
	1							
			3	4	6			2
	4	6			2		5	1
						3		6
				7			9	
	3	8	2					
	2							7
7					5	9		

Puzzle # 161 Hard

		9			8			
		8	3	5	6			9
6					7		2	
3		1		8	2		9	
			1		3			6
9			7					4
8				2			6	
	1							
2	5				4		1	

Puzzle # 162 Hard

	4					7	3	
6				4				
		5	3		7			1
	3	6						8
				8				4
						1	7	5
		2	8				5	
	6	4			3			
8			4	7		6	1	

Puzzle # 163 Hard

	7	3	8				1	
5		9	6					3
		2			1	6		
	4						3	8
		1		8			2	
7		8			6			
		6		3	2			
			5			9		
				7				

Puzzle # 164 Hard

	9	6						
8	4		7		9			5
3						1		
1		2						
	5					6	7	9
			4					
	1		5					
			6		2	5		
		3		1				8

Harmony Squares: LGBT Sudoku Series

Puzzle # 165 Hard

```
. . 9 | 1 . . | . 6 .
. 6 . | . 8 . | 7 . .
1 . . | . 7 . | 5 . .
------+-------+------
4 . 1 | . . . | . . .
. 7 . | 5 . . | . . 6
8 . . | 9 . 4 | . . .
------+-------+------
. 3 . | . . . | 2 1 .
. . . | . . . | 2 . .
. . . | . 9 8 | . . .
```

Puzzle # 166 Hard

```
. 8 3 | . 9 . | 2 . 5
. 2 . | . . . | 1 8 .
. 9 . | . . 6 | . . 4
------+-------+------
3 . . | . 8 . | . . .
. . 9 | . 3 . | . . 6
2 7 . | . . 5 | . . .
------+-------+------
. . . | 5 . . | . 1 .
7 . 6 | . 2 . | 5 . .
. . 1 | 8 7 . | . . .
```

Puzzle # 167 Hard

```
. 6 . | . 3 9 | . . .
4 . 9 | 2 . . | . . .
5 . 8 | . 6 . | . . 9
------+-------+------
. 5 . | 3 . 4 | . . .
6 . . | . 1 . | . . 8
. 1 3 | . . . | . . .
------+-------+------
3 8 . | . . 9 | . . 6
1 . 7 | . 6 . | . . .
. 2 . | 5 . 3 | 1 . 7
```

Puzzle # 168 Hard

```
. . 5 | . . 3 | 4 . .
. . 4 | 2 . . | . . 9
2 . . | . 6 . | . . 3
------+-------+------
. 5 6 | . . . | . . .
. 1 . | . . . | . . .
. . . | . . 8 | 1 . 2
------+-------+------
9 . . | . . 4 | . 3 .
. . . | 7 2 . | . . .
6 7 . | 5 . . | . . .
```

Puzzle # 169 Hard

7		3			5		8	
	6				7	1	5	
	9				3			7
	4		9			3		
8			4			7		
						5		
				9				1
	1		2				9	5
	2		8					

Puzzle # 170 Hard

9					1			
	3						4	
	8			6				3
7			3	9		2		
	2							
1	3		4			6	9	
8		6	9		2			
3		5	1					
			7	3	8			

Puzzle # 171 Hard

				4			9	3
3		9	5			7		
	4				6			
	3	4			2		7	6
		2	8				5	
9			4	6				
	2					4		
						5	3	7
			6	9		2		

Puzzle # 172 Hard

		8						2
8			2	7				
5	9		1	4				8
	1				5	4	2	
	5						1	3
			8					5
		7	1		6			
	1		6					9
2		5		3			8	

Puzzle # 173 Hard

```
. . . | 2 3 . | . . .
7 8 3 | 5 . . | . . .
. 5 2 | 4 . . | 6 . .
------+-------+------
. 3 . | 6 . . | 8 . .
4 . . | . 2 . | 5 6 .
6 . . | . 1 . | . . 2
------+-------+------
. 2 . | 4 . . | . . .
3 . 4 | . . . | 8 . .
. . . | . . 9 | 3 . 1
```

Puzzle # 174 Hard

```
6 . . | . 8 . | . . 5
8 1 . | 3 . . | . . .
. . . | . . . | 1 9 .
------+-------+------
3 6 . | . 5 . | 2 . .
. 9 5 | 2 . . | 6 . .
. 2 1 | 7 . 3 | . . .
------+-------+------
. 4 . | . . . | 2 . 6
. . . | . . . | 9 . 4
. 5 . | . 4 6 | . . 1
```

Puzzle # 175 Hard

```
. . . | . . . | . . 6
. 2 5 | 6 . 4 | . . 1
6 7 . | . . . | 8 . 9
------+-------+------
. . . | 7 . 5 | . 1 .
. 9 8 | 3 . . | 7 . .
1 . . | . . . | . . .
------+-------+------
5 . . | 9 . 4 | . . .
7 . . | . . 1 | . 5 .
. 8 1 | . . . | . . 4
```

Puzzle # 176 Hard

```
. . . | 6 . . | 9 . .
2 . 4 | . 3 . | . 5 .
. 1 . | . . 2 | . . 3
------+-------+------
4 . 3 | . . . | 8 5 .
. . . | . . . | . . .
7 8 . | . 6 9 | 1 . .
------+-------+------
8 4 . | 9 . . | . 1 .
. . 1 | 3 . . | 7 . 5
. 3 7 | 2 . . | . 6 .
```

Puzzle # 177 Hard

5		1			2			7
7	3				4		8	
9				8			2	
4		3				2		
8			4				9	
	6						7	4
					1	5		
2			7	9				
			3					

Puzzle # 178 Hard

1					5	3		
		4						5
						4	9	
	4		7				5	
6			3				2	4
5				4				6
2	9				3			7
	6			7				
7		1		8				2

Puzzle # 179 Hard

	9		7		5		6	
5		3			4			
			6	2	8			
		8	5					2
			2				4	
				8		9		
			8				7	3
9	3	5				6		
					9			

Puzzle # 180 Hard

8								
5		3			9		2	
	4		7		6		3	
	7	2			8			5
		9		7				
						1	9	
					5	9	8	
4	8					5		
	9		4					3

Harmony Squares: LGBT Sudoku Series

Puzzle # 181 Hard

7		4			2			1
2	1						4	
					1			3
	3		9			7		
9			4		7		5	
5	2	7	8				9	
	9			3		6		7
	5				6			4

Puzzle # 182 Hard

9		8			3	5		
	7			9	8			4
3								
			6	5				7
						8	6	
2			3	8		4	9	
5	3			4	9	1		
			7				5	
6	9	1						

Puzzle # 183 Hard

		5			7			
	7		8		2	9	6	
	1					3	5	
	7		4					
4			1			5	2	
9			5		4			
			8	3				
	2	3			5	7		
6		4			8			

Puzzle # 184 Hard

			6		7			
	9	4	8				2	
	3	5	9					
			8			2	9	
			2			1	6	
								3
						4	1	7
8							3	
	6			8				

Harmony Squares: LGBT Sudoku Series

Puzzle # 185 Hard

		4		8	6			7
	1	9		2		4		8
7	8				3			5
	5			3	1			
					2			
	2						9	3
9						3	6	
3						5	8	1
			3	1	6			

Puzzle # 186 Hard

	5	3						7
		7	3			9		8
	1		2	4				5
			9	2			8	6
2		8			1	7		
	7		8				5	
	8	5						2
3						5	1	
		6		2				

Puzzle # 187 Hard

1	9			2	7			
6		7		4	8	5		
3	1			2			9	
		4	9			3		
				8				5
7		1		4				8
	6	9		5				3
	4		2		6			9

Puzzle # 188 Hard

		6	7	1		9		
		7	5					6
5						8		
	6		1		4		9	
		8			5			
9	7	4	3				5	
				6				
6	4	9						
8						1		4

Puzzle # 189 Hard

8	7			3				
5	3	2				6	8	
	6				5		2	3
						8		
3			6	7			5	
	8		5	4	3			7
			3		9	4		
					2	5	7	
2			4			3		

Puzzle # 190 Hard

			5	4				
	5							
6			7	3			1	9
	6			8				
4			9			7		
	2					1	9	
1						4		
5			6	3				2
8			5	4			3	1

Puzzle # 191 Hard

	2			7		9		
								1
		5		1		2	6	
		8		2		7		
4	6	7	3			9		
		9				3		
1		4	7					
	9	2			3	1	4	
8			5				3	

Puzzle # 192 Hard

	9		6	2		5	8	
	2			5			3	4
5	4		8		3	6		2
			5	4	8			
			7		9	1	6	
6		8		1		3		9
4		9				2		6
	1						4	

Puzzle # 193 Hard

	8							
7				9			4	
	5	1			3			8
	9		4	7				2
	6							
5				2				9
8				6				7
9	4					6	2	
			3			4	8	

Puzzle # 194 Hard

	7			4				
			2	9	4			
		4	3		1		9	
	2			7			4	1
	5			8		9		
6	9		5					
7				1				
	1	6						7
9	3			7		8		4

Puzzle # 195 Hard

						2		
		9		2		8	7	
3				7	8			6
	5	7						
	8	3	2		7	4		
6			5		9			
	9		6					
						5	1	8
		1		8	3	9		2

Puzzle # 196 Hard

			6				9	
	2	4			1			3
5			4			1		
1	7			4				6
	5			1		3	7	
2		8		9				5
	1	2	8				3	
8		7	9		6		5	

Puzzle # 197 Hard

8								4
			3	6				8
						1	7	5
			4			7	3	
	3	7		5				1
4					6			
		3	6	4				
7	4				8	6	1	
	8			2			5	

Puzzle # 198 Hard

	4						1	
7		1		2	6			
9	8			1				
4	9			7		2		
2			3	4				1
8								
			6	8		2		
1			5		3			4
			4			6		

Puzzle # 199 Hard

			2			5		
2			8		1			
4		8						
			9				4	
			3		6			2
	7					1		
6		7			9		8	
			1					6
8	2			5			3	

Puzzle # 200 Hard

4					1		6	
		1						2
6								3
		3		4	7			
9		4	2					8
	8	6				1		
			7	2	4	8		
						2		
1							7	9

Harmony Squares: LGBT Sudoku Series

Puzzle # 201 Hard

				9	2	5		
	2	8						6
5			6		1			
			2					
	8	6						2
	4			1	9		8	
						7		
		7	8			1	9	
	7	5		3	6	2		

Puzzle # 202 Hard

8	1			2	7	4		
4			3		5			
				4		5		
5		8			6		4	
				3	2			9
	2			9	1			
	8					6	2	
	2	8					5	7
				4	8			

Puzzle # 203 Hard

			5	2		6		
		7						
	9	2	4					
		6				1		4
	7		4			9	5	
9	2				8			
	6				1		9	
			8				1	
		1		7		6		

Puzzle # 204 Hard

			3				8	9
		3					4	
6					2	3		7
		2	6		8			
	4			5	1			3
		6			4			
2			7				9	4
	3			4	1			2
								8

Puzzle # 205 Hard

						5		4
		5				6		
		8			6	1		
	8	2		3			9	
4		9			1		2	
7			2					
		6		5			7	
5			2					6
		7	1				5	9

Puzzle # 206 Hard

	3		2					5
4	2			6	1			
		5		9		2	6	
6						3		2
	9	3					7	
					6	4		
3			6		8			9
5							7	3
2			1	7		5		

Puzzle # 207 Hard

5		9		7		1		
7				6				5
		6	5				2	
	5	4						
	1			8	6			
6							5	
9			8	2				3
			7					2
2			4		9	1		

Puzzle # 208 Hard

			8	5	1			
	6						9	
		1	6	3		2		5
9						6	8	
	5	2	7			4	3	
	8	4						
		6	5		4			3
		3						
2				9		5		4

Puzzle # 209 Hard

		4	9	7			6	
1							3	
			6			7		
4		7	2					
2	1	9	3			5		7
								9
			3		4			
8		3	9					5
	4		5			3	9	6

Puzzle # 210 Hard

		3	9	7				
	9		5			1	2	
								3
1	2					9		8
8								
3			8	6		4	7	
	7		3					9
				6			1	7
6						2	3	

Harmony Squares: LGBT Sudoku Series

Solution Puzzle # 1

4	2	6	8	3	5	1	9	7
5	8	7	6	9	1	4	2	3
1	3	9	4	2	7	5	8	6
9	1	2	5	8	3	6	7	4
6	5	8	2	7	4	3	1	9
3	7	4	1	6	9	2	5	8
7	9	5	3	1	6	8	4	2
2	6	1	9	4	8	7	3	5
8	4	3	7	5	2	9	6	1

Solution Puzzle # 2

4	8	9	2	6	3	7	1	5
7	5	3	8	9	1	4	2	6
6	2	1	4	7	5	8	9	3
9	7	5	6	3	8	1	4	2
2	6	4	5	1	7	3	8	9
1	3	8	9	2	4	6	5	7
5	4	2	7	8	6	9	3	1
3	9	7	1	4	2	5	6	8
8	1	6	3	5	9	2	7	4

Solution Puzzle # 3

2	7	1	4	8	3	9	5	6
6	4	5	1	9	2	3	8	7
9	8	3	6	5	7	2	4	1
3	2	7	9	4	5	6	1	8
5	6	4	2	1	8	7	9	3
1	9	8	3	7	6	5	2	4
7	5	6	8	2	1	4	3	9
8	3	9	5	6	4	1	7	2
4	1	2	7	3	9	8	6	5

Solution Puzzle # 4

2	7	5	8	9	3	1	4	6
9	4	1	2	6	7	8	3	5
3	6	8	1	4	5	2	7	9
7	3	4	9	5	1	6	8	2
1	9	6	4	2	8	7	5	3
8	5	2	7	3	6	9	1	4
6	8	3	5	7	9	4	2	1
4	1	9	3	8	2	5	6	7
5	2	7	6	1	4	3	9	8

Solution Puzzle # 5

4	2	8	3	5	6	1	9	7
7	9	1	8	4	2	6	5	3
6	5	3	9	7	1	8	2	4
5	4	7	1	6	9	3	8	2
9	8	2	5	3	4	7	6	1
1	3	6	7	2	8	5	4	9
3	7	9	4	8	5	2	1	6
2	1	5	6	9	7	4	3	8
8	6	4	2	1	3	9	7	5

Solution Puzzle # 6

5	2	6	9	7	4	3	1	8
9	8	4	1	3	5	2	7	6
1	7	3	8	6	2	9	5	4
7	5	8	3	9	1	6	4	2
3	1	9	4	2	6	7	8	5
4	6	2	7	5	8	1	9	3
8	9	1	2	4	3	5	6	7
6	3	7	5	8	9	4	2	1
2	4	5	6	1	7	8	3	9

Solution Puzzle # 7

7	8	3	6	1	4	5	2	9
4	9	6	2	7	5	8	1	3
1	5	2	9	3	8	6	7	4
9	4	5	3	8	1	2	6	7
6	7	8	4	9	2	1	3	5
2	3	1	5	6	7	4	9	8
5	2	7	1	4	3	9	8	6
8	6	4	7	2	9	3	5	1
3	1	9	8	5	6	7	4	2

Solution Puzzle # 8

3	1	5	6	2	9	8	4	7
7	6	2	3	8	4	5	9	1
9	4	8	1	7	5	6	2	3
8	7	4	9	5	2	1	3	6
2	3	6	4	1	7	9	5	8
5	9	1	8	6	3	2	7	4
1	5	7	2	4	6	3	8	9
4	8	9	5	3	1	7	6	2
6	2	3	7	9	8	4	1	5

Solution Puzzle # 9

1	3	9	6	5	2	8	4	7
4	8	2	7	1	9	3	6	5
7	6	5	3	4	8	2	1	9
6	2	4	8	7	1	9	5	3
3	5	8	9	2	4	1	7	6
9	7	1	5	3	6	4	8	2
8	1	6	2	9	5	7	3	4
2	4	7	1	6	3	5	9	8
5	9	3	4	8	7	6	2	1

Solution Puzzle # 10

2	9	5	3	8	1	6	4	7
3	1	6	7	5	4	8	9	2
8	4	7	2	6	9	3	5	1
1	3	2	4	7	5	9	8	6
4	5	8	9	1	6	2	7	3
6	7	9	8	3	2	4	1	5
5	8	4	1	2	3	7	6	9
9	2	1	6	4	7	5	3	8
7	6	3	5	9	8	1	2	4

Solution Puzzle # 11

7	9	8	5	3	2	4	6	1
5	6	4	9	1	8	2	3	7
3	1	2	4	6	7	5	9	8
1	2	9	3	4	6	7	8	5
8	4	3	7	2	5	9	1	6
6	5	7	8	9	1	3	4	2
2	3	5	1	8	9	6	7	4
4	8	6	2	7	3	1	5	9
9	7	1	6	5	4	8	2	3

Solution Puzzle # 12

3	4	5	7	9	8	6	1	2
2	8	9	3	1	6	7	4	5
1	6	7	4	2	5	3	8	9
8	7	3	9	5	1	2	6	4
5	2	1	8	6	4	9	3	7
6	9	4	2	3	7	1	5	8
9	5	2	1	8	3	4	7	6
4	3	6	5	7	2	8	9	1
7	1	8	6	4	9	5	2	3

Harmony Squares: LGBT Sudoku Series

Solution Puzzle # 13

3	8	2	1	9	4	7	5	6
4	6	1	8	7	5	2	3	9
9	7	5	2	3	6	4	8	1
7	4	8	5	1	9	3	6	2
1	5	3	6	2	7	9	4	8
6	2	9	3	4	8	1	7	5
5	9	7	4	8	2	6	1	3
8	3	4	9	6	1	5	2	7
2	1	6	7	5	3	8	9	4

Solution Puzzle # 14

1	9	7	2	8	3	5	4	6
6	3	8	5	9	4	2	7	1
2	5	4	1	6	7	9	8	3
9	1	2	3	7	8	4	6	5
3	8	5	6	4	2	7	1	9
7	4	6	9	1	5	3	2	8
4	2	9	8	5	6	1	3	7
5	6	3	7	2	1	8	9	4
8	7	1	4	3	9	6	5	2

Solution Puzzle # 15

1	4	2	5	8	7	9	6	3
3	8	5	6	1	9	2	7	4
9	6	7	3	4	2	5	1	8
5	7	8	4	2	6	3	9	1
6	3	1	8	9	5	4	2	7
2	9	4	7	3	1	6	8	5
7	5	9	1	6	3	8	4	2
8	2	3	9	7	4	1	5	6
4	1	6	2	5	8	7	3	9

Solution Puzzle # 16

6	7	2	3	5	9	4	1	8
1	3	9	6	8	4	5	2	7
8	5	4	7	2	1	9	6	3
9	1	6	5	4	8	3	7	2
3	2	7	1	9	6	8	4	5
5	4	8	2	7	3	6	9	1
7	9	3	8	6	2	1	5	4
4	8	5	9	1	7	2	3	6
2	6	1	4	3	5	7	8	9

Solution Puzzle # 17

1	3	5	4	9	7	8	6	2
2	7	8	6	3	1	5	9	4
6	9	4	8	5	2	7	3	1
3	4	6	5	7	9	1	2	8
8	5	2	3	1	6	4	7	9
7	1	9	2	4	8	3	5	6
5	6	1	7	2	4	9	8	3
4	8	3	9	6	5	2	1	7
9	2	7	1	8	3	6	4	5

Solution Puzzle # 18

1	5	8	7	6	9	3	2	4
3	7	6	1	2	4	5	8	9
4	9	2	8	5	3	7	1	6
9	6	3	4	8	7	2	5	1
7	8	5	6	1	2	9	4	3
2	1	4	9	3	5	8	6	7
5	4	9	2	7	1	6	3	8
8	2	1	3	9	6	4	7	5
6	3	7	5	4	8	1	9	2

Harmony Squares: LGBT Sudoku Series

Solution Puzzle # 19

8	2	1	3	6	7	5	4	9
6	7	5	9	1	4	8	3	2
4	9	3	5	8	2	1	7	6
2	8	7	1	4	9	6	5	3
1	6	9	7	3	5	2	8	4
3	5	4	6	2	8	7	9	1
5	3	6	4	7	1	9	2	8
9	4	2	8	5	6	3	1	7
7	1	8	2	9	3	4	6	5

Solution Puzzle # 20

2	4	5	6	3	7	8	9	1
8	7	1	5	4	9	6	2	3
6	3	9	8	2	1	5	7	4
5	9	7	3	6	4	1	8	2
1	6	8	9	7	2	3	4	5
4	2	3	1	8	5	7	6	9
9	1	6	2	5	8	4	3	7
3	5	4	7	9	6	2	1	8
7	8	2	4	1	3	9	5	6

Solution Puzzle # 21

8	2	9	6	7	5	4	1	3
7	4	1	8	3	9	6	2	5
3	5	6	1	2	4	9	8	7
6	7	4	2	8	1	5	3	9
2	9	5	7	4	3	1	6	8
1	8	3	9	5	6	2	7	4
4	6	7	3	9	2	8	5	1
9	3	2	5	1	8	7	4	6
5	1	8	4	6	7	3	9	2

Solution Puzzle # 22

3	7	6	1	5	4	9	8	2
1	8	2	6	3	9	5	4	7
5	9	4	8	2	7	1	6	3
6	4	1	7	9	8	2	3	5
7	3	8	5	6	2	4	9	1
2	5	9	3	4	1	8	7	6
4	2	3	9	1	6	7	5	8
9	6	7	2	8	5	3	1	4
8	1	5	4	7	3	6	2	9

Solution Puzzle # 23

8	7	9	6	4	1	2	5	3
4	6	3	9	5	2	1	7	8
1	2	5	8	3	7	6	9	4
2	4	7	3	9	6	8	1	5
9	8	1	5	2	4	3	6	7
3	5	6	1	7	8	9	4	2
6	1	4	2	8	5	7	3	9
7	3	8	4	6	9	5	2	1
5	9	2	7	1	3	4	8	6

Solution Puzzle # 24

3	9	4	6	5	2	8	1	7
1	6	5	8	4	7	2	3	9
8	2	7	3	1	9	4	6	5
2	3	9	7	8	5	6	4	1
4	7	8	2	6	1	9	5	3
5	1	6	4	9	3	7	8	2
6	5	1	9	7	8	3	2	4
7	4	2	1	3	6	5	9	8
9	8	3	5	2	4	1	7	6

Harmony Squares: LGBT Sudoku Series

Solution Puzzle # 25

7	1	9	8	6	5	2	3	4
2	3	8	9	7	4	5	6	1
5	6	4	3	2	1	9	8	7
3	5	7	4	1	8	6	2	9
8	9	6	7	5	2	4	1	3
1	4	2	6	9	3	7	5	8
4	7	5	1	8	6	3	9	2
9	2	1	5	3	7	8	4	6
6	8	3	2	4	9	1	7	5

Solution Puzzle # 26

8	2	5	3	9	6	4	1	7
3	7	4	1	8	2	9	6	5
1	6	9	7	4	5	2	3	8
9	3	6	8	7	1	5	4	2
7	5	1	9	2	4	3	8	6
4	8	2	6	5	3	7	9	1
2	4	3	5	6	8	1	7	9
5	9	8	4	1	7	6	2	3
6	1	7	2	3	9	8	5	4

Solution Puzzle # 27

9	2	7	1	4	6	8	5	3
5	3	6	7	8	2	9	1	4
8	4	1	5	9	3	6	7	2
4	8	5	9	3	1	2	6	7
3	6	9	2	7	5	1	4	8
7	1	2	8	6	4	5	3	9
1	9	3	6	2	7	4	8	5
2	5	4	3	1	8	7	9	6
6	7	8	4	5	9	3	2	1

Solution Puzzle # 28

1	7	4	6	8	9	2	5	3
3	6	5	7	4	2	1	8	9
2	8	9	3	1	5	6	4	7
7	9	3	8	6	4	5	1	2
8	1	2	5	9	7	3	6	4
4	5	6	1	2	3	7	9	8
5	2	8	9	3	6	4	7	1
6	4	1	2	7	8	9	3	5
9	3	7	4	5	1	8	2	6

Solution Puzzle # 29

1	9	4	8	7	3	6	5	2
3	6	8	4	2	5	9	1	7
5	2	7	6	9	1	4	3	8
7	5	9	1	6	2	3	8	4
8	3	2	5	4	7	1	9	6
4	1	6	3	8	9	2	7	5
2	8	3	7	1	6	5	4	9
6	7	5	9	3	4	8	2	1
9	4	1	2	5	8	7	6	3

Solution Puzzle # 30

1	6	9	5	3	7	8	2	4
7	4	3	2	8	1	9	5	6
5	8	2	4	6	9	3	1	7
6	9	5	7	4	3	2	8	1
2	7	8	9	1	6	5	4	3
3	1	4	8	2	5	6	7	9
9	2	7	3	5	4	1	6	8
4	5	1	6	9	8	7	3	2
8	3	6	1	7	2	4	9	5

Harmony Squares: LGBT Sudoku Series

Solution Puzzle # 31

9	2	6	7	1	4	8	3	5
5	4	1	9	3	8	2	6	7
7	8	3	6	2	5	4	9	1
4	9	5	3	8	1	6	7	2
3	1	7	4	6	2	9	5	8
2	6	8	5	9	7	3	1	4
6	5	2	8	7	9	1	4	3
8	3	4	1	5	6	7	2	9
1	7	9	2	4	3	5	8	6

Solution Puzzle # 32

1	6	4	3	9	5	2	7	8
5	3	8	7	2	1	4	9	6
9	2	7	8	6	4	1	3	5
6	4	3	9	7	2	8	5	1
8	9	1	4	5	6	3	2	7
2	7	5	1	8	3	9	6	4
4	5	2	6	1	9	7	8	3
3	8	6	2	4	7	5	1	9
7	1	9	5	3	8	6	4	2

Solution Puzzle # 33

9	2	5	7	1	3	4	8	6
6	1	8	5	4	2	3	9	7
4	7	3	9	6	8	5	2	1
8	3	1	2	7	4	9	6	5
2	5	4	1	9	6	7	3	8
7	6	9	3	8	5	1	4	2
3	8	2	4	5	7	6	1	9
1	4	7	6	2	9	8	5	3
5	9	6	8	3	1	2	7	4

Solution Puzzle # 34

6	3	5	2	9	8	7	1	4
2	8	9	7	4	1	6	5	3
7	4	1	6	3	5	9	2	8
1	6	3	8	7	9	5	4	2
5	9	4	3	1	2	8	6	7
8	7	2	4	5	6	3	9	1
3	5	6	1	2	7	4	8	9
9	1	7	5	8	4	2	3	6
4	2	8	9	6	3	1	7	5

Solution Puzzle # 35

6	1	9	3	4	7	8	5	2
7	4	5	9	8	2	1	3	6
3	8	2	6	5	1	4	9	7
9	5	6	8	2	4	7	1	3
8	2	7	1	3	9	6	4	5
1	3	4	7	6	5	2	8	9
4	7	8	2	9	3	5	6	1
2	6	3	5	1	8	9	7	4
5	9	1	4	7	6	3	2	8

Solution Puzzle # 36

6	4	5	9	2	3	8	1	7
7	3	9	8	4	1	2	5	6
1	8	2	6	7	5	4	3	9
2	9	3	4	1	6	7	8	5
4	7	8	3	5	2	6	9	1
5	6	1	7	9	8	3	2	4
8	5	6	1	3	4	9	7	2
3	1	7	2	6	9	5	4	8
9	2	4	5	8	7	1	6	3

Harmony Squares: LGBT Sudoku Series

Solution Puzzle # 37

2	9	1	3	6	4	7	5	8
4	7	5	1	8	9	3	6	2
8	6	3	5	7	2	4	9	1
7	4	6	8	2	1	9	3	5
9	5	2	6	4	3	1	8	7
3	1	8	7	9	5	2	4	6
6	2	9	4	5	7	8	1	3
5	3	4	2	1	8	6	7	9
1	8	7	9	3	6	5	2	4

Solution Puzzle # 38

8	6	4	7	3	9	5	2	1
5	7	2	1	4	8	6	9	3
9	3	1	6	2	5	4	7	8
2	5	8	9	6	7	3	1	4
7	4	9	3	8	1	2	5	6
6	1	3	4	5	2	9	8	7
3	8	7	5	9	6	1	4	2
1	9	6	2	7	4	8	3	5
4	2	5	8	1	3	7	6	9

Solution Puzzle # 39

3	6	1	7	9	5	4	2	8
8	2	9	6	4	3	7	5	1
5	7	4	1	2	8	3	6	9
6	4	7	9	8	1	2	3	5
9	5	2	4	3	6	8	1	7
1	8	3	2	5	7	9	4	6
7	1	8	3	6	2	5	9	4
4	3	5	8	1	9	6	7	2
2	9	6	5	7	4	1	8	3

Solution Puzzle # 40

7	4	9	2	3	8	1	5	6
3	1	2	5	4	6	8	7	9
5	6	8	7	1	9	3	4	2
1	7	5	3	8	2	9	6	4
8	2	3	9	6	4	7	1	5
6	9	4	1	7	5	2	8	3
4	5	7	8	2	3	6	9	1
2	8	6	4	9	1	5	3	7
9	3	1	6	5	7	4	2	8

Solution Puzzle # 41

2	5	6	8	4	3	7	9	1
9	1	4	5	7	6	2	8	3
3	8	7	2	9	1	6	5	4
7	9	1	6	8	2	4	3	5
6	3	8	1	5	4	9	7	2
5	4	2	7	3	9	8	1	6
8	2	3	4	1	7	5	6	9
1	6	5	9	2	8	3	4	7
4	7	9	3	6	5	1	2	8

Solution Puzzle # 42

2	5	8	6	1	9	7	4	3
4	6	1	8	3	7	2	9	5
7	9	3	5	4	2	8	1	6
9	7	4	2	8	3	6	5	1
5	8	2	1	6	4	9	3	7
3	1	6	9	7	5	4	2	8
6	3	9	4	5	8	1	7	2
8	4	7	3	2	1	5	6	9
1	2	5	7	9	6	3	8	4

Harmony Squares: LGBT Sudoku Series

Solution Puzzle # 43

4	2	8	9	6	3	1	5	7
7	5	3	4	2	1	8	9	6
9	1	6	8	7	5	3	2	4
2	3	5	1	4	8	7	6	9
1	4	9	7	5	6	2	3	8
8	6	7	2	3	9	5	4	1
6	9	1	3	8	2	4	7	5
3	8	4	5	9	7	6	1	2
5	7	2	6	1	4	9	8	3

Solution Puzzle # 44

8	4	3	5	2	7	9	6	1
6	2	9	8	4	1	7	5	3
5	7	1	6	9	3	8	4	2
1	5	2	3	6	9	4	8	7
4	6	8	7	1	5	3	2	9
3	9	7	4	8	2	6	1	5
2	1	6	9	3	8	5	7	4
7	3	4	2	5	6	1	9	8
9	8	5	1	7	4	2	3	6

Solution Puzzle # 45

1	2	5	8	4	3	7	6	9
6	3	8	2	9	7	4	5	1
4	9	7	5	1	6	8	3	2
5	4	9	1	6	8	3	2	7
7	1	6	4	3	2	5	9	8
3	8	2	7	5	9	1	4	6
8	6	3	9	7	5	2	1	4
2	5	1	6	8	4	9	7	3
9	7	4	3	2	1	6	8	5

Solution Puzzle # 46

5	8	2	6	9	7	1	4	3
6	3	1	8	5	4	2	9	7
4	7	9	2	1	3	5	6	8
7	4	3	9	8	2	6	1	5
2	5	6	4	3	1	7	8	9
9	1	8	7	6	5	3	2	4
8	2	5	3	4	6	9	7	1
3	9	7	1	2	8	4	5	6
1	6	4	5	7	9	8	3	2

Solution Puzzle # 47

3	1	5	7	6	4	9	2	8
4	6	9	3	8	2	5	1	7
8	2	7	9	1	5	4	3	6
1	5	3	4	9	6	7	8	2
9	8	6	5	2	7	1	4	3
7	4	2	1	3	8	6	9	5
2	7	4	8	5	1	3	6	9
5	3	8	6	4	9	2	7	1
6	9	1	2	7	3	8	5	4

Solution Puzzle # 48

7	6	9	3	4	8	2	1	5
1	5	4	2	7	9	8	6	3
2	8	3	5	6	1	4	7	9
5	3	8	6	2	4	7	9	1
9	7	1	8	5	3	6	4	2
4	2	6	9	1	7	3	5	8
3	4	7	1	9	2	5	8	6
6	1	2	7	8	5	9	3	4
8	9	5	4	3	6	1	2	7

Harmony Squares: LGBT Sudoku Series

Solution Puzzle # 49

4	2	9	6	8	7	5	1	3
8	1	3	2	9	5	6	7	4
7	6	5	3	4	1	8	2	9
3	9	1	8	7	4	2	6	5
6	8	4	1	5	2	9	3	7
2	5	7	9	3	6	4	8	1
5	3	6	7	2	9	1	4	8
1	4	8	5	6	3	7	9	2
9	7	2	4	1	8	3	5	6

Solution Puzzle # 50

3	4	2	6	7	8	1	5	9
6	5	1	4	2	9	3	7	8
9	7	8	1	3	5	6	4	2
5	8	6	2	4	3	9	1	7
7	3	4	9	1	6	8	2	5
2	1	9	8	5	7	4	3	6
4	6	5	7	8	1	2	9	3
1	9	7	3	6	2	5	8	4
8	2	3	5	9	4	7	6	1

Solution Puzzle # 51

5	8	6	2	7	1	4	9	3
7	9	3	5	4	6	2	8	1
2	4	1	8	9	3	7	5	6
3	5	9	4	6	8	1	7	2
1	7	4	9	3	2	5	6	8
6	2	8	7	1	5	3	4	9
8	6	7	3	2	4	9	1	5
9	3	5	1	8	7	6	2	4
4	1	2	6	5	9	8	3	7

Solution Puzzle # 52

3	2	4	5	6	8	9	7	1
6	5	1	4	7	9	8	2	3
8	9	7	1	2	3	4	5	6
2	6	9	8	1	4	7	3	5
5	7	8	3	9	6	2	1	4
1	4	3	2	5	7	6	8	9
9	3	2	6	8	1	5	4	7
4	8	6	7	3	5	1	9	2
7	1	5	9	4	2	3	6	8

Solution Puzzle # 53

8	3	7	4	9	1	6	2	5
9	2	6	5	7	3	8	4	1
5	4	1	6	8	2	9	7	3
4	6	8	9	3	5	2	1	7
7	1	3	2	4	6	5	8	9
2	5	9	8	1	7	4	3	6
3	8	5	1	2	9	7	6	4
6	7	4	3	5	8	1	9	2
1	9	2	7	6	4	3	5	8

Solution Puzzle # 54

1	7	2	4	6	9	8	5	3
4	6	5	8	1	3	2	9	7
3	9	8	5	7	2	6	4	1
2	5	1	6	3	8	4	7	9
7	8	6	9	4	5	1	3	2
9	4	3	1	2	7	5	6	8
6	2	9	7	5	1	3	8	4
8	1	4	3	9	6	7	2	5
5	3	7	2	8	4	9	1	6

Harmony Squares: LGBT Sudoku Series

Solution Puzzle # 55

8	5	1	2	7	9	3	6	4
2	6	7	8	3	4	1	9	5
3	4	9	1	5	6	8	7	2
7	8	5	9	1	3	2	4	6
1	3	2	6	4	5	9	8	7
6	9	4	7	2	8	5	1	3
5	2	8	4	9	7	6	3	1
4	1	6	3	8	2	7	5	9
9	7	3	5	6	1	4	2	8

Solution Puzzle # 56

2	5	7	1	9	3	8	4	6
9	1	8	6	7	4	3	5	2
3	4	6	8	2	5	7	9	1
8	7	2	3	5	6	4	1	9
5	3	9	4	1	7	6	2	8
1	6	4	2	8	9	5	3	7
7	2	1	5	3	8	9	6	4
4	8	5	9	6	2	1	7	3
6	9	3	7	4	1	2	8	5

Solution Puzzle # 57

5	9	4	6	8	2	3	1	7
7	3	1	4	9	5	8	6	2
2	6	8	3	7	1	4	9	5
9	1	7	2	4	8	6	5	3
8	2	3	5	6	7	1	4	9
4	5	6	9	1	3	2	7	8
1	8	9	7	3	6	5	2	4
6	4	2	8	5	9	7	3	1
3	7	5	1	2	4	9	8	6

Solution Puzzle # 58

7	3	2	8	4	5	1	9	6
9	5	1	6	7	3	8	4	2
8	6	4	9	2	1	3	5	7
2	9	6	7	1	4	5	8	3
4	7	5	3	9	8	6	2	1
3	1	8	2	5	6	9	7	4
5	2	7	1	6	9	4	3	8
6	8	9	4	3	2	7	1	5
1	4	3	5	8	7	2	6	9

Solution Puzzle # 59

7	5	9	3	8	1	4	2	6
1	2	6	7	4	9	3	5	8
3	8	4	5	6	2	1	7	9
9	1	2	4	5	3	6	8	7
8	3	5	6	9	7	2	1	4
6	4	7	2	1	8	9	3	5
4	7	3	9	2	5	8	6	1
2	6	8	1	7	4	5	9	3
5	9	1	8	3	6	7	4	2

Solution Puzzle # 60

5	9	7	1	8	2	4	6	3
2	6	4	9	3	5	7	1	8
8	1	3	6	4	7	2	9	5
3	2	1	8	9	4	5	7	6
7	5	9	2	6	3	8	4	1
4	8	6	7	5	1	3	2	9
9	7	2	3	1	8	6	5	4
1	3	5	4	7	6	9	8	2
6	4	8	5	2	9	1	3	7

Harmony Squares: LGBT Sudoku Series

Solution Puzzle # 61

8	7	5	4	6	2	1	9	3
4	3	1	9	7	5	8	2	6
2	6	9	1	3	8	4	5	7
5	9	7	8	4	6	3	1	2
3	1	4	2	9	7	6	8	5
6	2	8	5	1	3	7	4	9
7	4	2	3	5	1	9	6	8
9	8	3	6	2	4	5	7	1
1	5	6	7	8	9	2	3	4

Solution Puzzle # 62

4	5	3	1	7	8	9	2	6
8	9	7	2	6	4	3	1	5
1	2	6	3	5	9	4	8	7
7	4	5	6	3	1	8	9	2
3	6	8	9	2	5	7	4	1
9	1	2	8	4	7	6	5	3
2	7	4	5	9	6	1	3	8
6	3	1	4	8	2	5	7	9
5	8	9	7	1	3	2	6	4

Solution Puzzle # 63

5	3	6	1	7	4	2	9	8
2	4	8	9	6	5	1	3	7
9	1	7	2	8	3	5	6	4
7	5	4	6	1	9	3	8	2
6	2	9	8	3	7	4	1	5
3	8	1	4	5	2	6	7	9
8	7	5	3	2	1	9	4	6
1	9	2	7	4	6	8	5	3
4	6	3	5	9	8	7	2	1

Solution Puzzle # 64

2	6	4	8	7	5	3	9	1
3	7	8	9	1	2	4	6	5
9	5	1	6	4	3	7	8	2
4	8	2	7	9	1	6	5	3
6	9	7	3	5	8	1	2	4
1	3	5	2	6	4	9	7	8
8	2	9	4	3	7	5	1	6
7	1	3	5	8	6	2	4	9
5	4	6	1	2	9	8	3	7

Solution Puzzle # 65

9	6	5	3	8	2	4	1	7
3	2	8	4	1	7	9	5	6
4	7	1	5	9	6	2	3	8
5	8	6	2	4	3	1	7	9
7	9	3	1	5	8	6	2	4
1	4	2	6	7	9	3	8	5
8	3	9	7	2	4	5	6	1
6	5	4	8	3	1	7	9	2
2	1	7	9	6	5	8	4	3

Solution Puzzle # 66

8	6	4	5	7	1	3	2	9
3	9	1	6	8	2	7	4	5
7	5	2	9	4	3	6	8	1
9	1	3	8	6	7	2	5	4
5	2	6	1	9	4	8	7	3
4	7	8	3	2	5	1	9	6
2	3	9	7	5	6	4	1	8
6	8	7	4	1	9	5	3	2
1	4	5	2	3	8	9	6	7

Harmony Squares: LGBT Sudoku Series

Solution Puzzle # 67

4	6	8	7	1	9	5	3	2
9	7	1	2	3	5	4	6	8
3	2	5	6	8	4	1	7	9
1	8	9	3	4	2	6	5	7
7	5	4	9	6	8	2	1	3
6	3	2	5	7	1	8	9	4
5	9	6	8	2	3	7	4	1
2	1	7	4	9	6	3	8	5
8	4	3	1	5	7	9	2	6

Solution Puzzle # 68

3	7	9	6	8	5	1	2	4
6	2	4	7	9	1	5	8	3
5	8	1	4	3	2	7	6	9
7	3	8	9	1	6	4	5	2
1	5	2	8	4	3	9	7	6
4	9	6	5	2	7	3	1	8
9	1	5	2	6	4	8	3	7
8	6	7	3	5	9	2	4	1
2	4	3	1	7	8	6	9	5

Solution Puzzle # 69

5	4	8	1	9	2	6	7	3
9	1	3	4	6	7	5	8	2
7	6	2	8	3	5	9	1	4
6	2	5	7	8	4	1	3	9
1	8	7	9	5	3	2	4	6
3	9	4	2	1	6	8	5	7
2	3	6	5	7	1	4	9	8
8	7	1	6	4	9	3	2	5
4	5	9	3	2	8	7	6	1

Solution Puzzle # 70

6	4	8	7	5	1	3	9	2
1	3	2	8	9	4	5	6	7
9	7	5	2	6	3	8	1	4
5	1	3	4	7	6	9	2	8
2	9	7	3	1	8	6	4	5
8	6	4	5	2	9	1	7	3
3	8	1	6	4	7	2	5	9
7	5	9	1	8	2	4	3	6
4	2	6	9	3	5	7	8	1

Solution Puzzle # 71

6	5	3	1	8	7	4	9	2
7	1	2	4	6	9	3	8	5
4	9	8	5	2	3	1	7	6
9	3	5	7	4	2	6	1	8
8	7	6	9	3	1	5	2	4
2	4	1	8	5	6	9	3	7
1	2	4	6	9	8	7	5	3
3	6	9	2	7	5	8	4	1
5	8	7	3	1	4	2	6	9

Solution Puzzle # 72

9	1	3	4	8	5	6	7	2
6	7	5	3	1	2	9	8	4
8	4	2	9	7	6	3	1	5
1	2	6	5	4	7	8	3	9
4	9	8	2	3	1	5	6	7
3	5	7	8	6	9	4	2	1
7	8	1	6	9	4	2	5	3
2	6	4	7	5	3	1	9	8
5	3	9	1	2	8	7	4	6

Solution Puzzle # 73

6	5	3	1	8	7	4	2	9
1	9	8	6	4	2	7	5	3
2	7	4	3	5	9	8	6	1
5	8	2	7	9	3	6	1	4
7	3	9	4	6	1	2	8	5
4	1	6	8	2	5	9	3	7
8	2	5	9	1	4	3	7	6
9	6	7	5	3	8	1	4	2
3	4	1	2	7	6	5	9	8

Solution Puzzle # 74

1	4	6	7	9	3	8	5	2
7	5	9	1	2	8	4	6	3
2	8	3	6	5	4	1	9	7
4	9	2	8	3	5	6	7	1
8	1	5	2	7	6	3	4	9
3	6	7	9	4	1	2	8	5
5	2	4	3	6	9	7	1	8
9	3	8	4	1	7	5	2	6
6	7	1	5	8	2	9	3	4

Solution Puzzle # 75

1	3	9	8	2	6	7	5	4
5	8	7	4	3	1	2	6	9
6	2	4	5	7	9	3	1	8
8	5	6	9	1	2	4	3	7
9	7	2	3	5	4	6	8	1
3	4	1	6	8	7	9	2	5
2	9	5	7	6	8	1	4	3
4	1	3	2	9	5	8	7	6
7	6	8	1	4	3	5	9	2

Solution Puzzle # 76

6	5	7	4	9	8	3	1	2
8	3	9	1	2	7	6	5	4
1	4	2	5	6	3	7	9	8
2	7	5	6	1	9	4	8	3
3	8	1	7	4	5	2	6	9
4	9	6	3	8	2	5	7	1
9	6	4	2	7	1	8	3	5
5	2	8	9	3	6	1	4	7
7	1	3	8	5	4	9	2	6

Solution Puzzle # 77

1	7	3	6	2	8	5	9	4
8	2	9	7	5	4	6	1	3
6	4	5	3	1	9	2	7	8
2	6	8	9	4	7	1	3	5
9	5	4	1	6	3	8	2	7
7	3	1	2	8	5	4	6	9
5	9	6	8	7	1	3	4	2
4	1	7	5	3	2	9	8	6
3	8	2	4	9	6	7	5	1

Solution Puzzle # 78

9	2	1	8	7	3	4	5	6
7	8	6	4	5	1	2	9	3
3	4	5	2	9	6	1	7	8
6	5	3	1	2	8	9	4	7
4	1	2	9	3	7	8	6	5
8	7	9	5	6	4	3	2	1
2	3	8	6	4	5	7	1	9
5	9	7	3	1	2	6	8	4
1	6	4	7	8	9	5	3	2

Solution Puzzle # 79

4	1	3	6	9	5	7	2	8
9	8	2	3	4	7	5	6	1
5	7	6	1	2	8	3	4	9
3	6	7	2	5	1	9	8	4
8	4	1	9	6	3	2	5	7
2	9	5	8	7	4	1	3	6
6	5	9	4	1	2	8	7	3
1	2	8	7	3	6	4	9	5
7	3	4	5	8	9	6	1	2

Solution Puzzle # 80

7	5	6	2	1	9	3	8	4
8	9	3	7	6	4	5	2	1
4	2	1	8	5	3	7	9	6
1	8	7	3	4	5	9	6	2
2	6	5	9	8	7	4	1	3
3	4	9	6	2	1	8	5	7
9	1	2	4	7	8	6	3	5
5	3	4	1	9	6	2	7	8
6	7	8	5	3	2	1	4	9

Solution Puzzle # 81

9	7	4	2	5	1	3	6	8
1	6	8	7	3	9	2	5	4
2	5	3	6	8	4	9	7	1
7	1	2	3	4	5	8	9	6
4	8	5	9	1	6	7	2	3
6	3	9	8	2	7	4	1	5
3	2	6	5	9	8	1	4	7
5	9	1	4	7	3	6	8	2
8	4	7	1	6	2	5	3	9

Solution Puzzle # 82

7	4	2	5	3	8	9	6	1
8	1	5	6	9	2	3	4	7
9	3	6	4	7	1	8	5	2
2	8	7	3	4	9	6	1	5
1	6	9	2	5	7	4	8	3
4	5	3	8	1	6	2	7	9
3	2	4	7	6	5	1	9	8
5	9	8	1	2	4	7	3	6
6	7	1	9	8	3	5	2	4

Solution Puzzle # 83

1	4	3	8	7	5	2	6	9
2	7	9	6	3	1	5	8	4
5	6	8	2	9	4	3	1	7
3	1	7	4	8	9	6	2	5
9	2	6	7	5	3	1	4	8
8	5	4	1	6	2	9	7	3
4	9	2	3	1	8	7	5	6
7	3	1	5	4	6	8	9	2
6	8	5	9	2	7	4	3	1

Solution Puzzle # 84

8	4	3	7	5	1	9	6	2
5	1	7	6	9	2	3	4	8
9	6	2	8	3	4	7	1	5
6	9	4	1	2	3	8	5	7
7	2	8	9	6	5	4	3	1
3	5	1	4	7	8	6	2	9
4	3	5	2	8	9	1	7	6
2	8	6	3	1	7	5	9	4
1	7	9	5	4	6	2	8	3

Harmony Squares: LGBT Sudoku Series

Solution Puzzle # 85

2	6	7	9	3	4	5	1	8
4	1	5	8	7	6	3	2	9
9	8	3	2	1	5	4	7	6
5	4	9	7	8	1	6	3	2
8	3	6	5	2	9	7	4	1
7	2	1	4	6	3	8	9	5
3	7	2	1	5	8	9	6	4
1	9	8	6	4	7	2	5	3
6	5	4	3	9	2	1	8	7

Solution Puzzle # 86

4	8	1	3	5	2	6	9	7
6	5	9	7	1	4	3	2	8
3	2	7	9	6	8	1	4	5
9	3	2	6	7	5	8	1	4
8	7	6	4	9	1	5	3	2
5	1	4	2	8	3	7	6	9
7	6	3	5	2	9	4	8	1
1	9	5	8	4	6	2	7	3
2	4	8	1	3	7	9	5	6

Solution Puzzle # 87

2	1	3	7	9	8	4	5	6
4	6	8	5	1	2	9	7	3
7	9	5	4	3	6	1	8	2
6	4	9	3	7	1	8	2	5
8	3	1	2	6	5	7	9	4
5	2	7	9	8	4	3	6	1
1	5	2	8	4	9	6	3	7
9	7	6	1	5	3	2	4	8
3	8	4	6	2	7	5	1	9

Solution Puzzle # 88

4	7	8	3	1	6	2	9	5
1	3	6	5	9	2	7	4	8
9	5	2	8	4	7	6	1	3
3	6	9	4	7	8	1	5	2
2	1	4	6	3	5	8	7	9
5	8	7	1	2	9	4	3	6
6	4	1	9	8	3	5	2	7
8	2	3	7	5	1	9	6	4
7	9	5	2	6	4	3	8	1

Solution Puzzle # 89

7	1	5	8	2	3	9	4	6
9	2	6	1	4	7	5	8	3
3	4	8	6	5	9	1	2	7
1	7	3	4	8	2	6	9	5
5	8	2	9	1	6	3	7	4
4	6	9	7	3	5	2	1	8
2	3	1	5	7	4	8	6	9
8	9	7	3	6	1	4	5	2
6	5	4	2	9	8	7	3	1

Solution Puzzle # 90

6	9	8	5	7	4	2	1	3
7	5	1	3	6	2	8	9	4
4	3	2	8	1	9	6	5	7
9	4	6	1	2	7	3	8	5
5	1	7	4	8	3	9	2	6
2	8	3	9	5	6	7	4	1
3	2	5	7	9	1	4	6	8
1	7	9	6	4	8	5	3	2
8	6	4	2	3	5	1	7	9

Harmony Squares: LGBT Sudoku Series

Solution Puzzle # 91

7	3	2	4	9	5	6	1	8
5	1	6	8	3	2	9	4	7
9	8	4	1	6	7	5	3	2
1	4	5	7	8	6	2	9	3
2	6	7	3	5	9	1	8	4
8	9	3	2	4	1	7	5	6
4	7	9	6	1	3	8	2	5
6	5	8	9	2	4	3	7	1
3	2	1	5	7	8	4	6	9

Solution Puzzle # 92

8	4	3	6	1	5	9	7	2
6	7	5	9	4	2	1	3	8
9	1	2	7	8	3	5	6	4
7	9	8	4	2	1	3	5	6
4	3	6	5	7	8	2	1	9
2	5	1	3	6	9	8	4	7
3	2	4	1	9	7	6	8	5
1	6	9	8	5	4	7	2	3
5	8	7	2	3	6	4	9	1

Solution Puzzle # 93

3	4	5	2	8	6	7	9	1
7	6	2	9	3	1	4	5	8
1	9	8	4	7	5	2	3	6
8	7	4	5	1	9	6	2	3
2	3	1	7	6	4	5	8	9
9	5	6	8	2	3	1	4	7
6	8	7	3	4	2	9	1	5
5	2	3	1	9	7	8	6	4
4	1	9	6	5	8	3	7	2

Solution Puzzle # 94

6	4	3	5	8	2	1	7	9
1	5	2	6	9	7	4	3	8
7	9	8	4	3	1	6	5	2
9	8	4	7	1	3	2	6	5
5	1	7	2	4	6	9	8	3
3	2	6	9	5	8	7	1	4
8	7	1	3	2	9	5	4	6
4	6	9	8	7	5	3	2	1
2	3	5	1	6	4	8	9	7

Solution Puzzle # 95

5	3	1	7	8	4	6	2	9
2	6	4	9	1	3	7	5	8
9	8	7	6	2	5	1	4	3
4	2	8	1	9	7	3	6	5
3	1	9	4	5	6	8	7	2
7	5	6	8	3	2	4	9	1
6	9	3	2	7	1	5	8	4
8	7	5	3	4	9	2	1	6
1	4	2	5	6	8	9	3	7

Solution Puzzle # 96

2	6	8	4	7	5	9	3	1
5	1	3	2	6	9	8	4	7
7	9	4	1	3	8	2	5	6
6	7	2	5	9	4	1	8	3
8	4	5	6	1	3	7	2	9
9	3	1	8	2	7	4	6	5
3	2	6	9	8	1	5	7	4
4	8	9	7	5	6	3	1	2
1	5	7	3	4	2	6	9	8

Harmony Squares: LGBT Sudoku Series

Solution Puzzle # 97

8	4	5	2	9	1	7	3	6
1	3	2	7	5	6	9	4	8
7	6	9	8	3	4	2	1	5
2	5	1	4	8	9	3	6	7
9	8	6	3	2	7	1	5	4
3	7	4	6	1	5	8	2	9
5	2	3	9	6	8	4	7	1
6	9	7	1	4	3	5	8	2
4	1	8	5	7	2	6	9	3

Solution Puzzle # 98

4	5	9	2	1	3	8	7	6
6	8	3	4	7	5	1	2	9
2	1	7	6	8	9	5	3	4
9	6	4	3	5	2	7	8	1
8	7	5	1	6	4	2	9	3
3	2	1	8	9	7	4	6	5
1	3	2	7	4	6	9	5	8
5	4	6	9	2	8	3	1	7
7	9	8	5	3	1	6	4	2

Solution Puzzle # 99

8	2	7	6	3	9	5	4	1
1	3	5	2	4	7	9	6	8
4	9	6	1	5	8	3	7	2
6	7	4	5	8	2	1	9	3
3	5	8	9	6	1	4	2	7
9	1	2	3	7	4	6	8	5
5	8	9	4	2	3	7	1	6
7	4	3	8	1	6	2	5	9
2	6	1	7	9	5	8	3	4

Solution Puzzle # 100

2	8	4	6	9	1	7	3	5
9	3	6	2	5	7	4	8	1
1	5	7	4	3	8	2	6	9
5	2	8	9	6	4	1	7	3
3	7	9	5	1	2	6	4	8
6	4	1	8	7	3	9	5	2
7	9	3	1	8	6	5	2	4
8	1	2	7	4	5	3	9	6
4	6	5	3	2	9	8	1	7

Solution Puzzle # 101

9	8	4	1	3	2	5	7	6
1	7	6	8	4	5	2	9	3
2	5	3	9	6	7	4	1	8
8	2	5	7	9	1	3	6	4
7	3	9	4	5	6	1	8	2
4	6	1	2	8	3	9	5	7
3	9	8	5	7	4	6	2	1
6	1	7	3	2	9	8	4	5
5	4	2	6	1	8	7	3	9

Solution Puzzle # 102

1	9	6	7	5	4	8	3	2
3	2	8	9	6	1	7	5	4
7	5	4	3	2	8	1	9	6
2	6	7	1	8	5	9	4	3
8	4	5	2	9	3	6	1	7
9	1	3	4	7	6	5	2	8
5	8	1	6	4	2	3	7	9
6	7	2	5	3	9	4	8	1
4	3	9	8	1	7	2	6	5

Harmony Squares: LGBT Sudoku Series

Solution Puzzle # 103

4	3	1	9	8	5	7	6	2
5	6	8	4	7	2	9	3	1
9	2	7	6	1	3	8	4	5
6	8	9	1	4	7	5	2	3
7	4	5	3	2	6	1	8	9
2	1	3	5	9	8	6	7	4
1	7	2	8	5	4	3	9	6
3	5	4	7	6	9	2	1	8
8	9	6	2	3	1	4	5	7

Solution Puzzle # 104

5	9	7	8	3	4	1	2	6
3	4	8	2	1	6	5	7	9
2	1	6	5	7	9	8	3	4
4	6	5	9	2	7	3	1	8
8	2	1	4	5	3	6	9	7
9	7	3	1	6	8	4	5	2
1	3	9	6	4	2	7	8	5
6	5	2	7	8	1	9	4	3
7	8	4	3	9	5	2	6	1

Solution Puzzle # 105

2	3	8	4	7	9	5	1	6
9	5	4	1	2	6	7	8	3
6	1	7	8	5	3	2	4	9
4	2	9	6	1	5	3	7	8
7	6	3	2	9	8	4	5	1
1	8	5	7	3	4	6	9	2
3	9	1	5	6	7	8	2	4
5	4	6	9	8	2	1	3	7
8	7	2	3	4	1	9	6	5

Solution Puzzle # 106

8	4	1	3	9	7	6	5	2
5	7	2	1	6	8	3	9	4
9	6	3	4	5	2	1	8	7
6	2	5	8	3	1	7	4	9
7	8	9	5	4	6	2	1	3
1	3	4	2	7	9	8	6	5
4	9	7	6	1	3	5	2	8
2	5	6	7	8	4	9	3	1
3	1	8	9	2	5	4	7	6

Solution Puzzle # 107

5	8	4	7	2	6	1	9	3
1	3	2	8	9	4	7	6	5
7	9	6	3	1	5	8	4	2
2	1	3	4	5	7	9	8	6
6	5	8	1	3	9	4	2	7
4	7	9	2	6	8	5	3	1
3	4	1	5	8	2	6	7	9
9	2	7	6	4	1	3	5	8
8	6	5	9	7	3	2	1	4

Solution Puzzle # 108

4	5	8	1	3	2	7	9	6
7	2	9	5	6	4	8	1	3
3	6	1	9	7	8	5	2	4
8	4	3	6	9	7	1	5	2
1	9	6	2	5	3	4	7	8
2	7	5	4	8	1	3	6	9
6	3	7	8	2	5	9	4	1
9	8	4	7	1	6	2	3	5
5	1	2	3	4	9	6	8	7

Solution Puzzle # 109

9	6	7	2	1	8	5	3	4
2	1	4	5	6	3	7	9	8
3	8	5	9	7	4	6	2	1
1	5	2	3	4	7	8	6	9
4	7	6	8	9	1	2	5	3
8	3	9	6	5	2	1	4	7
6	4	8	1	2	9	3	7	5
5	9	3	7	8	6	4	1	2
7	2	1	4	3	5	9	8	6

Solution Puzzle # 110

3	5	9	6	1	8	7	2	4
6	4	8	2	3	7	9	5	1
7	1	2	4	9	5	8	3	6
4	3	1	5	7	6	2	9	8
2	9	5	8	4	3	6	1	7
8	7	6	9	2	1	3	4	5
1	2	7	3	8	4	5	6	9
9	6	4	7	5	2	1	8	3
5	8	3	1	6	9	4	7	2

Solution Puzzle # 111

9	2	7	3	6	4	5	8	1
6	1	4	5	7	8	9	3	2
5	8	3	1	2	9	4	6	7
1	9	8	2	3	5	7	4	6
7	5	2	9	4	6	8	1	3
3	4	6	8	1	7	2	9	5
2	6	9	4	5	3	1	7	8
8	3	1	7	9	2	6	5	4
4	7	5	6	8	1	3	2	9

Solution Puzzle # 112

1	2	8	9	6	7	5	4	3
3	5	9	4	1	2	7	6	8
7	4	6	8	5	3	9	1	2
6	9	2	7	8	1	4	3	5
4	7	3	5	2	6	1	8	9
8	1	5	3	9	4	2	7	6
5	8	1	6	4	9	3	2	7
9	3	4	2	7	8	6	5	1
2	6	7	1	3	5	8	9	4

Solution Puzzle # 113

4	3	6	7	9	1	2	8	5
7	8	1	4	2	5	3	6	9
9	5	2	3	8	6	1	4	7
8	9	5	6	1	3	4	7	2
2	1	7	9	5	4	8	3	6
3	6	4	8	7	2	9	5	1
6	2	3	1	4	7	5	9	8
1	7	8	5	3	9	6	2	4
5	4	9	2	6	8	7	1	3

Solution Puzzle # 114

1	8	3	9	2	5	7	4	6
6	4	5	7	8	3	2	9	1
9	2	7	1	6	4	3	8	5
4	9	1	8	5	2	6	7	3
3	5	8	6	7	1	9	2	4
2	7	6	4	3	9	5	1	8
5	6	4	2	9	8	1	3	7
7	1	9	3	4	6	8	5	2
8	3	2	5	1	7	4	6	9

Harmony Squares: LGBT Sudoku Series

Solution Puzzle # 115

2	6	4	1	8	9	3	7	5
3	1	7	2	6	5	4	8	9
5	8	9	4	7	3	6	2	1
4	9	1	8	3	7	2	5	6
7	5	2	6	4	1	8	9	3
6	3	8	9	5	2	1	4	7
9	4	5	3	2	6	7	1	8
1	2	3	7	9	8	5	6	4
8	7	6	5	1	4	9	3	2

Solution Puzzle # 116

5	7	4	6	8	3	9	1	2
3	1	2	4	5	9	6	8	7
9	8	6	2	1	7	4	5	3
8	2	9	5	4	6	7	3	1
6	4	7	1	3	2	8	9	5
1	3	5	7	9	8	2	6	4
7	9	8	3	2	1	5	4	6
4	6	1	8	7	5	3	2	9
2	5	3	9	6	4	1	7	8

Solution Puzzle # 117

7	2	5	6	9	1	8	4	3
1	6	8	3	4	7	9	2	5
9	4	3	2	8	5	6	7	1
3	1	2	9	6	8	7	5	4
8	5	7	4	1	3	2	9	6
6	9	4	7	5	2	1	3	8
5	7	9	1	3	6	4	8	2
4	8	6	5	2	9	3	1	7
2	3	1	8	7	4	5	6	9

Solution Puzzle # 118

6	8	9	5	1	3	2	7	4
7	2	4	6	9	8	3	5	1
3	5	1	4	2	7	6	8	9
1	7	5	3	4	9	8	2	6
2	4	6	8	5	1	9	3	7
9	3	8	2	7	6	4	1	5
5	6	2	7	3	4	1	9	8
8	1	3	9	6	5	7	4	2
4	9	7	1	8	2	5	6	3

Solution Puzzle # 119

5	3	7	4	8	1	9	2	6
1	8	4	6	9	2	5	7	3
9	6	2	5	3	7	8	4	1
7	9	3	2	5	6	4	1	8
2	4	8	7	1	9	6	3	5
6	5	1	8	4	3	2	9	7
8	7	5	3	2	4	1	6	9
3	2	9	1	6	8	7	5	4
4	1	6	9	7	5	3	8	2

Solution Puzzle # 120

9	4	8	5	7	6	1	2	3
3	5	2	1	4	8	6	7	9
6	1	7	3	2	9	5	8	4
7	6	4	9	3	5	8	1	2
1	3	5	2	8	7	4	9	6
2	8	9	4	6	1	3	5	7
4	2	1	7	5	3	9	6	8
8	9	3	6	1	2	7	4	5
5	7	6	8	9	4	2	3	1

Solution Puzzle # 121

5	7	4	1	8	9	3	2	6
3	9	8	5	2	6	4	7	1
6	2	1	3	7	4	8	5	9
1	4	5	7	9	8	2	6	3
7	8	6	2	5	3	9	1	4
9	3	2	6	4	1	7	8	5
2	5	3	9	1	7	6	4	8
4	1	9	8	6	2	5	3	7
8	6	7	4	3	5	1	9	2

Solution Puzzle # 122

2	3	7	1	8	5	9	4	6
4	5	6	7	9	2	1	3	8
8	1	9	6	3	4	2	5	7
3	6	8	5	2	9	4	7	1
1	4	5	8	7	6	3	2	9
9	7	2	4	1	3	6	8	5
7	8	4	3	6	1	5	9	2
5	2	1	9	4	7	8	6	3
6	9	3	2	5	8	7	1	4

Solution Puzzle # 123

8	7	6	4	2	5	3	1	9
1	4	9	8	7	3	5	2	6
3	5	2	9	6	1	7	8	4
6	2	7	1	3	8	4	9	5
4	9	1	2	5	6	8	3	7
5	8	3	7	9	4	1	6	2
9	3	5	6	8	7	2	4	1
2	1	8	5	4	9	6	7	3
7	6	4	3	1	2	9	5	8

Solution Puzzle # 124

4	1	5	8	9	6	3	7	2
3	9	7	5	2	4	1	8	6
8	6	2	1	3	7	4	9	5
9	7	4	3	5	1	6	2	8
6	2	1	9	4	8	5	3	7
5	8	3	7	6	2	9	1	4
1	4	6	2	7	9	8	5	3
2	3	8	4	1	5	7	6	9
7	5	9	6	8	3	2	4	1

Solution Puzzle # 125

5	6	2	8	7	1	9	3	4
4	9	7	5	6	3	2	8	1
8	1	3	4	2	9	7	6	5
1	8	6	3	9	5	4	2	7
7	2	9	6	8	4	1	5	3
3	5	4	7	1	2	6	9	8
2	7	8	1	5	6	3	4	9
9	3	5	2	4	7	8	1	6
6	4	1	9	3	8	5	7	2

Solution Puzzle # 126

6	8	1	7	4	5	9	2	3
2	4	7	3	6	9	5	1	8
3	9	5	1	8	2	6	4	7
8	5	2	6	7	3	4	9	1
9	1	4	2	5	8	7	3	6
7	3	6	9	1	4	8	5	2
4	7	9	8	2	1	3	6	5
5	2	8	4	3	6	1	7	9
1	6	3	5	9	7	2	8	4

Harmony Squares: LGBT Sudoku Series

Solution Puzzle # 127

2	3	6	4	7	1	8	9	5
7	8	1	3	9	5	4	2	6
4	9	5	6	8	2	3	1	7
6	4	3	7	2	8	1	5	9
1	7	2	5	4	9	6	3	8
9	5	8	1	3	6	2	7	4
5	2	9	8	6	3	7	4	1
3	6	4	9	1	7	5	8	2
8	1	7	2	5	4	9	6	3

Solution Puzzle # 128

7	4	2	8	5	3	9	1	6
1	9	6	4	7	2	5	8	3
5	8	3	9	1	6	7	4	2
6	2	8	3	9	7	4	5	1
3	5	1	6	4	8	2	7	9
9	7	4	5	2	1	6	3	8
2	1	9	7	8	5	3	6	4
4	3	7	1	6	9	8	2	5
8	6	5	2	3	4	1	9	7

Solution Puzzle # 129

4	1	8	7	9	2	5	6	3
6	5	9	1	3	8	7	2	4
7	2	3	6	4	5	1	8	9
8	3	6	5	7	9	4	1	2
5	4	2	8	1	3	9	7	6
1	9	7	2	6	4	3	5	8
3	8	5	9	2	7	6	4	1
2	6	4	3	5	1	8	9	7
9	7	1	4	8	6	2	3	5

Solution Puzzle # 130

7	6	9	3	4	2	5	8	1
8	2	3	1	5	6	7	9	4
1	4	5	9	8	7	3	6	2
2	9	4	7	3	8	1	5	6
6	1	7	5	9	4	8	2	3
3	5	8	2	6	1	4	7	9
4	7	2	8	1	9	6	3	5
5	8	6	4	2	3	9	1	7
9	3	1	6	7	5	2	4	8

Solution Puzzle # 131

1	5	6	9	2	8	3	7	4
2	7	8	1	4	3	5	6	9
4	3	9	5	6	7	8	1	2
5	4	2	6	9	1	7	3	8
3	6	1	7	8	4	2	9	5
9	8	7	2	3	5	6	4	1
8	9	5	3	1	6	4	2	7
6	1	4	8	7	2	9	5	3
7	2	3	4	5	9	1	8	6

Solution Puzzle # 132

4	7	1	9	6	5	8	3	2
8	2	9	1	3	7	4	6	5
3	5	6	4	2	8	1	9	7
5	9	3	8	7	6	2	1	4
6	8	7	2	1	4	9	5	3
2	1	4	3	5	9	6	7	8
9	6	2	5	8	3	7	4	1
7	3	8	6	4	1	5	2	9
1	4	5	7	9	2	3	8	6

Solution Puzzle # 133

9	3	4	7	1	5	8	2	6
7	6	8	2	9	3	4	5	1
1	5	2	8	4	6	9	7	3
4	7	5	6	2	1	3	9	8
8	9	1	3	7	4	5	6	2
3	2	6	9	5	8	1	4	7
6	8	7	4	3	9	2	1	5
5	4	3	1	6	2	7	8	9
2	1	9	5	8	7	6	3	4

Solution Puzzle # 134

7	1	4	8	3	2	6	5	9
2	6	3	7	5	9	1	4	8
9	5	8	4	1	6	7	3	2
5	4	2	6	9	8	3	7	1
8	3	9	1	7	4	2	6	5
1	7	6	3	2	5	9	8	4
3	9	7	5	8	1	4	2	6
4	8	1	2	6	3	5	9	7
6	2	5	9	4	7	8	1	3

Solution Puzzle # 135

3	1	9	6	4	8	5	7	2
7	5	2	9	3	1	6	8	4
8	6	4	7	5	2	3	9	1
9	8	3	2	1	7	4	5	6
4	7	5	3	8	6	2	1	9
1	2	6	5	9	4	8	3	7
6	3	1	8	2	9	7	4	5
2	4	8	1	7	5	9	6	3
5	9	7	4	6	3	1	2	8

Solution Puzzle # 136

8	4	2	7	5	3	9	6	1
9	5	6	1	8	2	3	7	4
1	3	7	6	9	4	2	5	8
4	7	5	2	1	8	6	9	3
6	9	8	3	4	7	5	1	2
2	1	3	5	6	9	8	4	7
5	2	4	9	3	1	7	8	6
7	8	9	4	2	6	1	3	5
3	6	1	8	7	5	4	2	9

Solution Puzzle # 137

6	4	2	8	7	1	3	9	5
1	3	8	5	2	9	4	6	7
9	7	5	3	4	6	8	1	2
2	1	3	6	5	7	9	8	4
5	9	7	1	8	4	6	2	3
8	6	4	9	3	2	5	7	1
4	8	6	7	1	3	2	5	9
3	5	1	2	9	8	7	4	6
7	2	9	4	6	5	1	3	8

Solution Puzzle # 138

8	4	7	1	5	2	6	9	3
5	2	1	6	3	9	8	4	7
9	6	3	4	7	8	1	5	2
6	1	9	5	8	3	7	2	4
2	3	4	9	1	7	5	6	8
7	5	8	2	6	4	9	3	1
4	7	6	8	2	5	3	1	9
3	9	5	7	4	1	2	8	6
1	8	2	3	9	6	4	7	5

Harmony Squares: LGBT Sudoku Series

Solution Puzzle # 139

3	2	4	6	8	9	5	1	7
9	6	5	4	7	1	3	2	8
1	8	7	5	2	3	4	6	9
4	9	8	1	3	5	6	7	2
6	3	1	7	9	2	8	5	4
7	5	2	8	6	4	1	9	3
5	7	3	9	4	6	2	8	1
8	4	6	2	1	7	9	3	5
2	1	9	3	5	8	7	4	6

Solution Puzzle # 140

3	6	2	4	8	7	1	5	9
1	9	8	3	5	2	4	6	7
5	7	4	9	1	6	3	8	2
7	3	9	8	6	1	5	2	4
8	4	1	2	3	5	9	7	6
2	5	6	7	4	9	8	3	1
4	1	5	6	7	3	2	9	8
9	8	7	5	2	4	6	1	3
6	2	3	1	9	8	7	4	5

Solution Puzzle # 141

3	8	5	4	2	7	1	6	9
7	1	6	9	3	5	2	8	4
9	4	2	6	8	1	5	7	3
4	3	8	2	9	6	7	5	1
2	5	7	1	4	3	8	9	6
1	6	9	7	5	8	3	4	2
8	2	1	5	6	4	9	3	7
6	7	3	8	1	9	4	2	5
5	9	4	3	7	2	6	1	8

Solution Puzzle # 142

5	4	3	2	7	9	8	6	1
8	6	2	4	5	1	7	3	9
7	9	1	8	3	6	4	2	5
3	1	6	5	9	7	2	8	4
4	8	9	1	2	3	5	7	6
2	7	5	6	8	4	1	9	3
1	3	8	9	4	2	6	5	7
6	2	7	3	1	5	9	4	8
9	5	4	7	6	8	3	1	2

Solution Puzzle # 143

8	3	5	6	9	1	2	7	4
9	6	1	2	4	7	3	5	8
4	2	7	3	8	5	6	9	1
6	5	8	4	2	3	7	1	9
3	7	4	9	1	6	5	8	2
1	9	2	5	7	8	4	3	6
5	1	3	8	6	4	9	2	7
2	8	6	7	3	9	1	4	5
7	4	9	1	5	2	8	6	3

Solution Puzzle # 144

2	9	8	3	6	1	4	7	5
1	5	3	8	7	4	9	2	6
7	4	6	2	5	9	1	3	8
6	8	9	1	2	3	5	4	7
3	7	2	4	8	5	6	9	1
5	1	4	6	9	7	2	8	3
4	2	1	7	3	6	8	5	9
9	6	7	5	4	8	3	1	2
8	3	5	9	1	2	7	6	4

Solution Puzzle # 145

2	6	4	7	8	1	5	3	9
3	1	7	5	9	6	8	4	2
5	8	9	4	3	2	1	6	7
6	5	2	9	4	8	7	1	3
7	9	3	1	6	5	4	2	8
1	4	8	2	7	3	6	9	5
9	3	6	8	1	7	2	5	4
4	7	5	6	2	9	3	8	1
8	2	1	3	5	4	9	7	6

Solution Puzzle # 146

1	9	3	8	2	7	4	5	6
7	4	8	6	5	3	2	9	1
2	5	6	9	1	4	3	7	8
9	7	5	1	4	8	6	2	3
8	2	4	7	3	6	5	1	9
3	6	1	5	9	2	8	4	7
6	1	2	3	7	5	9	8	4
4	8	9	2	6	1	7	3	5
5	3	7	4	8	9	1	6	2

Solution Puzzle # 147

7	2	4	3	8	5	1	6	9
6	9	8	7	2	1	5	4	3
1	3	5	9	4	6	8	7	2
9	6	1	2	7	8	4	3	5
3	8	7	6	5	4	9	2	1
5	4	2	1	9	3	6	8	7
8	7	3	5	6	9	2	1	4
4	1	9	8	3	2	7	5	6
2	5	6	4	1	7	3	9	8

Solution Puzzle # 148

8	5	7	1	6	4	9	3	2
6	3	9	7	2	8	1	4	5
4	1	2	3	5	9	7	8	6
7	4	8	2	3	5	6	1	9
1	2	6	9	4	7	3	5	8
3	9	5	6	8	1	4	2	7
5	7	1	8	9	3	2	6	4
9	6	4	5	1	2	8	7	3
2	8	3	4	7	6	5	9	1

Solution Puzzle # 149

8	3	4	1	7	5	9	6	2
7	5	9	6	2	8	1	3	4
1	6	2	3	4	9	5	7	8
3	8	7	5	9	1	4	2	6
9	2	6	8	3	4	7	5	1
4	1	5	2	6	7	3	8	9
2	9	8	7	1	3	6	4	5
6	7	1	4	5	2	8	9	3
5	4	3	9	8	6	2	1	7

Solution Puzzle # 150

4	9	3	2	7	5	6	1	8
7	1	6	3	8	9	5	4	2
2	8	5	4	6	1	7	9	3
1	7	2	5	4	6	3	8	9
6	3	9	7	1	8	2	5	4
5	4	8	9	3	2	1	6	7
3	5	7	6	9	4	8	2	1
8	6	4	1	2	3	9	7	5
9	2	1	8	5	7	4	3	6

Solution Puzzle # 151

2	1	8	7	3	4	9	6	5
7	9	6	8	1	5	2	3	4
5	3	4	2	6	9	1	8	7
4	6	2	1	8	3	5	7	9
8	7	1	5	9	6	4	2	3
9	5	3	4	7	2	6	1	8
3	8	5	6	4	1	7	9	2
6	4	7	9	2	8	3	5	1
1	2	9	3	5	7	8	4	6

Solution Puzzle # 152

8	3	2	7	9	5	6	4	1
5	7	1	3	4	6	2	8	9
4	6	9	1	8	2	7	5	3
1	2	7	5	6	8	9	3	4
6	4	5	9	7	3	1	2	8
3	9	8	2	1	4	5	7	6
2	1	4	8	5	9	3	6	7
9	8	3	6	2	7	4	1	5
7	5	6	4	3	1	8	9	2

Solution Puzzle # 153

5	3	8	7	9	2	6	4	1
9	7	6	1	4	8	5	3	2
1	2	4	5	3	6	7	8	9
3	6	9	2	7	1	4	5	8
4	1	2	8	5	3	9	6	7
7	8	5	9	6	4	2	1	3
8	5	1	6	2	9	3	7	4
2	4	7	3	8	5	1	9	6
6	9	3	4	1	7	8	2	5

Solution Puzzle # 154

6	8	2	1	4	9	7	3	5
9	3	1	5	8	7	2	4	6
5	7	4	6	2	3	9	1	8
3	2	7	4	6	1	5	8	9
8	1	9	2	7	5	3	6	4
4	6	5	3	9	8	1	2	7
1	9	6	7	3	4	8	5	2
7	4	3	8	5	2	6	9	1
2	5	8	9	1	6	4	7	3

Solution Puzzle # 155

9	7	1	8	2	5	3	4	6
2	4	6	1	3	7	9	8	5
8	5	3	4	6	9	1	2	7
7	3	5	6	1	8	4	9	2
6	9	4	2	7	3	8	5	1
1	2	8	5	9	4	7	6	3
3	8	2	7	4	6	5	1	9
5	1	9	3	8	2	6	7	4
4	6	7	9	5	1	2	3	8

Solution Puzzle # 156

6	7	9	8	2	5	4	3	1
8	1	2	7	3	4	5	6	9
4	5	3	1	6	9	7	8	2
2	8	7	5	9	6	3	1	4
1	4	6	2	8	3	9	7	5
3	9	5	4	7	1	8	2	6
9	2	1	3	5	7	6	4	8
5	3	8	6	4	2	1	9	7
7	6	4	9	1	8	2	5	3

Harmony Squares: LGBT Sudoku Series

Solution Puzzle # 157

2	6	9	7	4	5	8	3	1
3	5	8	9	1	2	4	7	6
1	4	7	8	3	6	9	5	2
5	2	3	4	8	1	7	6	9
6	9	1	3	5	7	2	8	4
7	8	4	6	2	9	3	1	5
8	3	6	1	9	4	5	2	7
9	7	5	2	6	3	1	4	8
4	1	2	5	7	8	6	9	3

Solution Puzzle # 158

4	9	1	2	3	7	6	5	8
2	8	5	9	6	1	7	4	3
6	3	7	5	8	4	2	9	1
9	7	3	6	2	8	5	1	4
1	4	8	7	5	9	3	2	6
5	2	6	4	1	3	9	8	7
7	5	4	8	9	6	1	3	2
8	1	9	3	7	2	4	6	5
3	6	2	1	4	5	8	7	9

Solution Puzzle # 159

2	9	1	5	6	3	4	8	7
5	8	4	7	9	2	3	6	1
7	6	3	8	1	4	9	2	5
3	4	6	1	7	8	5	9	2
8	1	7	9	2	5	6	3	4
9	5	2	3	4	6	1	7	8
1	2	9	4	3	7	8	5	6
6	3	8	2	5	1	7	4	9
4	7	5	6	8	9	2	1	3

Solution Puzzle # 160

6	5	4	1	2	9	8	7	3
2	1	3	7	5	8	6	4	9
8	9	7	3	4	6	5	1	2
3	4	6	9	8	2	7	5	1
9	7	2	5	1	4	3	8	6
1	8	5	6	7	3	2	9	4
4	3	8	2	9	7	1	6	5
5	2	9	8	6	1	4	3	7
7	6	1	4	3	5	9	2	8

Solution Puzzle # 161

4	7	9	2	1	8	6	5	3
1	2	8	3	5	6	4	7	9
6	3	5	9	4	7	8	2	1
3	6	1	4	8	2	7	9	5
5	4	7	1	9	3	2	8	6
9	8	2	7	6	5	1	3	4
8	9	4	5	2	1	3	6	7
7	1	6	8	3	9	5	4	2
2	5	3	6	7	4	9	1	8

Solution Puzzle # 162

9	4	1	5	2	8	7	3	6
6	7	3	9	4	1	5	8	2
2	8	5	3	6	7	9	4	1
5	3	6	7	1	4	2	9	8
1	9	7	2	8	5	3	6	4
4	2	8	6	3	9	1	7	5
3	1	2	8	9	6	4	5	7
7	6	4	1	5	3	8	2	9
8	5	9	4	7	2	6	1	3

Solution Puzzle # 163

6	7	3	8	4	5	2	1	9
5	1	9	6	2	7	8	4	3
4	8	2	3	9	1	5	6	7
9	4	5	2	1	6	7	3	8
3	6	1	7	8	9	4	2	5
7	2	8	4	5	3	6	9	1
8	5	6	9	3	2	1	7	4
1	3	7	5	6	4	9	8	2
2	9	4	1	7	8	3	5	6

Solution Puzzle # 164

2	9	6	1	3	5	8	4	7
8	4	1	7	6	9	3	2	5
3	7	5	2	4	8	9	1	6
1	6	2	8	9	7	4	5	3
4	5	8	3	2	1	6	7	9
7	3	9	4	5	6	1	8	2
6	1	7	5	8	3	2	9	4
9	8	4	6	7	2	5	3	1
5	2	3	9	1	4	7	6	8

Solution Puzzle # 165

7	4	9	1	5	3	8	6	2
3	6	5	2	8	9	7	4	1
1	8	2	4	7	6	9	5	3
4	2	1	8	6	7	3	9	5
9	7	3	5	2	1	4	8	6
8	5	6	9	3	4	1	2	7
6	3	8	7	4	5	2	1	9
5	9	4	3	1	2	6	7	8
2	1	7	6	9	8	5	3	4

Solution Puzzle # 166

4	8	3	1	9	7	2	6	5
6	2	7	4	5	3	1	8	9
1	9	5	2	8	6	3	7	4
3	6	4	9	1	8	7	5	2
5	1	9	7	3	2	8	4	6
2	7	8	6	4	5	9	3	1
8	3	2	5	6	9	4	1	7
7	4	6	3	2	1	5	9	8
9	5	1	8	7	4	6	2	3

Solution Puzzle # 167

2	6	1	8	3	9	7	5	4
4	7	9	2	5	1	8	6	3
5	3	8	4	6	7	2	1	9
8	5	2	3	9	4	6	7	1
6	9	4	7	1	5	3	2	8
7	1	3	6	2	8	4	9	5
3	8	5	1	7	2	9	4	6
1	4	7	9	8	6	5	3	2
9	2	6	5	4	3	1	8	7

Solution Puzzle # 168

1	6	5	8	9	3	4	2	7
7	3	4	2	1	5	6	8	9
2	8	9	4	6	7	5	1	3
3	5	6	1	4	2	9	7	8
8	1	2	9	7	6	3	5	4
4	9	7	3	5	8	1	6	2
9	2	1	6	8	4	7	3	5
5	4	3	7	2	1	8	9	6
6	7	8	5	3	9	2	4	1

Harmony Squares: LGBT Sudoku Series

Solution Puzzle # 169

7	4	3	2	1	5	9	8	6
2	6	8	9	4	7	1	5	3
1	9	5	8	6	3	4	2	7
5	1	4	7	9	2	3	6	8
8	3	9	4	5	6	7	1	2
6	2	7	1	3	8	5	4	9
4	8	6	5	7	9	2	3	1
3	7	1	6	2	4	8	9	5
9	5	2	3	8	1	6	7	4

Solution Puzzle # 170

9	5	7	3	4	1	2	8	6
6	2	3	5	8	7	1	4	9
4	8	1	2	9	6	7	5	3
7	6	4	1	3	9	5	2	8
5	9	2	7	6	8	4	3	1
1	3	8	4	2	5	6	9	7
8	1	6	9	5	2	3	7	4
3	7	5	8	1	4	9	6	2
2	4	9	6	7	3	8	1	5

Solution Puzzle # 171

2	8	5	7	4	1	6	9	3
3	6	9	5	2	8	7	4	1
7	4	1	9	3	6	8	2	5
8	3	4	1	5	2	9	7	6
6	1	2	8	7	9	3	5	4
9	5	7	4	6	3	1	8	2
5	2	8	3	1	7	4	6	9
1	9	6	2	8	4	5	3	7
4	7	3	6	9	5	2	1	8

Solution Puzzle # 172

1	7	6	8	5	3	9	4	2
8	4	3	9	2	7	5	6	1
5	9	2	1	4	6	3	7	8
7	8	1	3	9	5	4	2	6
6	5	9	2	7	4	8	1	3
3	2	4	6	8	1	7	9	5
9	3	8	7	1	2	6	5	4
4	1	7	5	6	8	2	3	9
2	6	5	4	3	9	1	8	7

Solution Puzzle # 173

1	4	6	7	2	3	5	9	8
7	8	3	9	5	6	1	2	4
9	5	2	1	4	8	7	6	3
2	3	9	5	6	4	8	1	7
4	1	8	3	7	2	9	5	6
6	7	5	8	9	1	4	3	2
8	2	1	4	3	5	6	7	9
3	9	4	6	1	7	2	8	5
5	6	7	2	8	9	3	4	1

Solution Puzzle # 174

6	7	9	1	2	8	4	3	5
8	1	4	5	3	9	7	6	2
5	3	2	6	7	4	8	1	9
3	6	8	4	9	5	1	2	7
7	9	5	2	8	1	6	4	3
4	2	1	7	6	3	5	9	8
9	4	3	8	1	7	2	5	6
1	8	6	3	5	2	9	7	4
2	5	7	9	4	6	3	8	1

Harmony Squares: LGBT Sudoku Series

Solution Puzzle # 175

8	1	3	9	2	7	5	4	6
9	2	5	6	8	4	3	7	1
6	7	4	1	5	3	8	2	9
3	6	2	7	9	5	4	1	8
4	9	8	3	1	2	7	6	5
1	5	7	4	6	8	2	9	3
5	3	9	2	4	6	1	8	7
7	4	6	8	3	1	9	5	2
2	8	1	5	7	9	6	3	4

Solution Puzzle # 176

3	7	8	6	4	5	9	2	1
2	9	4	7	3	1	6	5	8
6	1	5	8	9	2	4	7	3
4	6	3	1	2	8	5	9	7
1	5	9	4	7	3	2	8	6
7	8	2	5	6	9	1	3	4
8	4	6	9	5	7	3	1	2
9	2	1	3	8	6	7	4	5
5	3	7	2	1	4	8	6	9

Solution Puzzle # 177

5	8	1	9	3	2	4	6	7
7	3	2	6	1	4	9	8	5
9	4	6	5	8	7	1	2	3
4	9	3	1	7	6	2	5	8
8	2	7	4	5	3	6	9	1
1	6	5	8	2	9	3	7	4
3	7	8	2	6	1	5	4	9
2	1	4	7	9	5	8	3	6
6	5	9	3	4	8	7	1	2

Solution Puzzle # 178

1	7	4	2	9	5	3	6	8
9	8	6	4	3	1	2	7	5
3	2	5	8	6	7	4	9	1
8	4	9	7	2	6	1	5	3
6	1	7	3	5	8	9	2	4
5	3	2	1	4	9	7	8	6
2	9	8	6	1	3	5	4	7
4	6	3	5	7	2	8	1	9
7	5	1	9	8	4	6	3	2

Solution Puzzle # 179

8	9	2	7	1	5	3	6	4
5	6	3	9	8	4	2	1	7
4	7	1	3	6	2	8	5	9
1	4	8	5	9	6	7	3	2
6	5	9	2	7	3	1	4	8
3	2	7	1	4	8	5	9	6
2	1	6	8	5	9	4	7	3
9	3	5	4	2	7	6	8	1
7	8	4	6	3	1	9	2	5

Solution Puzzle # 180

8	6	7	2	1	3	4	5	9
5	1	3	8	4	9	7	2	6
2	4	9	7	5	6	8	3	1
9	7	2	1	6	8	3	4	5
1	5	4	9	3	7	2	6	8
6	3	8	5	2	4	1	9	7
3	2	1	6	7	5	9	8	4
4	8	6	3	9	1	5	7	2
7	9	5	4	8	2	6	1	3

Harmony Squares: LGBT Sudoku Series

Solution Puzzle # 181

7	3	4	9	5	2	8	6	1
2	1	5	3	6	8	7	4	9
6	8	9	7	4	1	5	2	3
8	4	3	6	9	5	1	7	2
9	6	1	4	2	7	3	5	8
5	2	7	8	1	3	4	9	6
4	7	6	1	8	9	2	3	5
1	9	2	5	3	4	6	8	7
3	5	8	2	7	6	9	1	4

Solution Puzzle # 182

9	6	8	4	2	3	5	7	1
1	7	2	5	9	8	6	3	4
3	4	5	1	7	6	2	8	9
4	8	9	6	5	2	3	1	7
7	5	3	9	1	4	8	6	2
2	1	6	3	8	7	4	9	5
5	3	7	8	4	9	1	2	6
8	2	4	7	6	1	9	5	3
6	9	1	2	3	5	7	4	8

Solution Puzzle # 183

3	2	6	5	9	4	7	1	8
5	4	7	1	8	3	2	9	6
8	9	1	6	7	2	4	3	5
2	7	5	9	4	6	1	8	3
4	6	3	8	1	7	9	5	2
9	1	8	2	3	5	6	4	7
7	5	9	4	2	8	3	6	1
1	8	2	3	6	9	5	7	4
6	3	4	7	5	1	8	2	9

Solution Puzzle # 184

2	8	1	6	5	7	3	4	9
6	9	4	8	1	3	7	2	5
7	3	5	9	4	2	8	6	1
3	1	8	5	7	6	2	9	4
9	5	2	4	3	1	6	7	8
4	7	6	2	9	8	5	1	3
5	2	9	3	6	4	1	8	7
8	4	7	1	2	5	9	3	6
1	6	3	7	8	9	4	5	2

Solution Puzzle # 185

2	3	5	4	9	8	6	1	7
6	1	9	5	2	7	4	3	8
7	8	4	1	6	3	9	2	5
8	5	6	9	3	1	7	4	2
4	9	3	8	7	2	1	5	6
1	2	7	6	5	4	8	9	3
9	7	1	2	8	5	3	6	4
3	6	2	7	4	9	5	8	1
5	4	8	3	1	6	2	7	9

Solution Puzzle # 186

4	5	3	9	8	6	1	2	7
6	2	7	3	1	5	9	4	8
8	1	9	2	4	7	3	6	5
5	3	1	7	9	2	4	8	6
2	6	8	4	5	1	7	3	9
9	7	4	8	6	3	2	5	1
7	8	5	1	3	4	6	9	2
3	9	2	6	7	8	5	1	4
1	4	6	5	2	9	8	7	3

Harmony Squares: LGBT Sudoku Series

Solution Puzzle # 187

1	9	5	6	8	2	7	3	4
6	3	7	1	9	4	8	5	2
4	8	2	5	7	3	9	6	1
3	1	8	7	2	5	4	9	6
5	2	4	9	6	1	3	8	7
9	7	6	4	3	8	2	1	5
7	5	1	3	4	9	6	2	8
2	6	9	8	5	7	1	4	3
8	4	3	2	1	6	5	7	9

Solution Puzzle # 188

4	8	6	7	1	3	9	2	5
3	9	7	5	2	8	4	1	6
5	1	2	6	4	9	7	8	3
2	6	5	1	7	4	3	9	8
1	3	8	2	9	5	6	4	7
9	7	4	3	8	6	2	5	1
7	5	1	4	6	2	8	3	9
6	4	9	8	3	1	5	7	2
8	2	3	9	5	7	1	6	4

Solution Puzzle # 189

8	7	1	2	3	6	9	4	5
5	3	2	7	9	4	6	8	1
9	6	4	1	8	5	7	2	3
7	4	5	9	2	1	8	3	6
3	2	9	8	6	7	1	5	4
1	8	6	5	4	3	2	9	7
6	5	8	3	7	9	4	1	2
4	9	3	6	1	2	5	7	8
2	1	7	4	5	8	3	6	9

Solution Puzzle # 190

2	9	3	1	5	4	6	8	7
7	5	1	8	9	6	3	2	4
6	8	4	2	7	3	5	1	9
9	7	6	3	1	8	2	4	5
4	1	8	9	2	5	7	6	3
3	2	5	4	6	7	1	9	8
1	3	2	7	8	9	4	5	6
5	4	9	6	3	1	8	7	2
8	6	7	5	4	2	9	3	1

Solution Puzzle # 191

6	2	1	8	4	7	5	9	3
9	4	3	2	6	5	7	8	1
7	8	5	9	3	1	4	2	6
3	5	8	1	9	2	6	7	4
4	6	7	3	5	8	9	1	2
2	1	9	4	7	6	3	5	8
1	3	4	7	2	9	8	6	5
5	9	2	6	8	3	1	4	7
8	7	6	5	1	4	2	3	9

Solution Puzzle # 192

7	9	3	4	6	2	5	8	1
8	2	6	9	5	1	7	3	4
5	4	1	8	7	3	6	9	2
1	6	7	5	4	8	9	2	3
2	8	4	7	3	9	1	6	5
9	3	5	1	2	6	4	7	8
6	7	8	2	1	4	3	5	9
4	5	9	3	8	7	2	1	6
3	1	2	6	9	5	8	4	7

Harmony Squares: LGBT Sudoku Series

Solution Puzzle # 193

4	8	9	5	1	7	2	3	6
7	3	6	8	9	2	1	4	5
2	5	1	6	4	3	7	9	8
3	9	8	4	7	6	5	1	2
1	6	2	9	3	5	8	7	4
5	7	4	1	2	8	3	6	9
8	1	3	2	6	4	9	5	7
9	4	5	7	8	1	6	2	3
6	2	7	3	5	9	4	8	1

Solution Puzzle # 194

5	7	9	6	4	8	1	3	2
1	6	3	7	2	9	4	8	5
2	8	4	3	5	1	7	9	6
3	2	8	9	6	7	5	4	1
4	5	7	1	8	2	9	6	3
6	9	1	5	3	4	2	7	8
7	4	2	8	1	3	6	5	9
8	1	6	4	9	5	3	2	7
9	3	5	2	7	6	8	1	4

Solution Puzzle # 195

8	7	4	1	5	6	2	9	3
1	6	9	3	2	4	8	7	5
3	2	5	9	7	8	1	4	6
4	5	7	8	3	1	6	2	9
9	8	3	2	6	7	4	5	1
6	1	2	5	4	9	3	8	7
2	9	8	6	1	5	7	3	4
7	3	6	4	9	2	5	1	8
5	4	1	7	8	3	9	6	2

Solution Puzzle # 196

7	8	1	3	6	2	5	9	4
9	2	4	5	7	1	8	6	3
5	3	6	4	8	9	1	2	7
1	7	3	2	4	5	9	8	6
4	5	9	6	1	8	3	7	2
2	6	8	7	9	3	4	1	5
6	1	2	8	5	4	7	3	9
3	9	5	1	2	7	6	4	8
8	4	7	9	3	6	2	5	1

Solution Puzzle # 197

8	2	5	9	7	1	3	6	4
1	7	4	3	6	5	2	9	8
3	6	9	2	8	4	1	7	5
2	5	8	4	1	9	7	3	6
6	3	7	8	5	2	9	4	1
4	9	1	7	3	6	5	8	2
5	1	3	6	4	7	8	2	9
7	4	2	5	9	8	6	1	3
9	8	6	1	2	3	4	5	7

Solution Puzzle # 198

6	4	2	7	3	5	9	1	8
7	3	1	9	8	2	6	4	5
9	8	5	6	1	4	3	7	2
4	9	3	8	7	1	2	5	6
2	5	7	3	4	6	8	9	1
8	1	6	2	5	9	4	3	7
3	7	4	1	6	8	5	2	9
1	6	9	5	2	3	7	8	4
5	2	8	4	9	7	1	6	3

Solution Puzzle # 199

7	6	9	2	4	3	5	1	8
2	3	5	8	6	1	4	9	7
4	1	8	7	9	5	6	2	3
1	8	6	9	7	2	3	4	5
5	9	4	3	1	6	8	7	2
3	7	2	5	8	4	1	6	9
6	5	7	4	3	9	2	8	1
9	4	3	1	2	8	7	5	6
8	2	1	6	5	7	9	3	4

Solution Puzzle # 200

4	2	8	3	5	1	9	6	7
5	3	1	6	7	9	4	8	2
6	9	7	4	8	2	5	1	3
2	1	3	8	4	7	6	9	5
9	5	4	2	1	6	7	3	8
7	8	6	9	3	5	1	2	4
3	6	9	7	2	4	8	5	1
8	7	5	1	9	3	2	4	6
1	4	2	5	6	8	3	7	9

Solution Puzzle # 201

8	6	1	3	9	2	5	7	4
4	9	2	8	5	7	3	1	6
5	3	7	6	4	1	8	2	9
7	5	9	2	6	8	4	3	1
1	8	6	4	7	3	9	5	2
2	4	3	5	1	9	6	8	7
3	1	8	9	2	4	7	6	5
6	2	4	7	8	5	1	9	3
9	7	5	1	3	6	2	4	8

Solution Puzzle # 202

8	1	5	9	2	7	4	3	6
4	7	6	3	1	5	2	9	8
2	3	9	6	4	8	5	7	1
5	9	8	1	7	6	3	4	2
1	6	4	5	3	2	7	8	9
7	2	3	4	8	9	1	6	5
9	8	1	7	5	3	6	2	4
3	4	2	8	6	1	9	5	7
6	5	7	2	9	4	8	1	3

Solution Puzzle # 203

1	4	3	8	5	2	7	6	9
5	8	6	7	1	9	3	4	2
7	9	2	4	6	3	5	8	1
8	3	5	6	9	7	1	2	4
6	1	7	2	4	8	9	5	3
9	2	4	1	3	5	8	7	6
3	6	8	5	2	1	4	9	7
4	7	9	3	8	6	2	1	5
2	5	1	9	7	4	6	3	8

Solution Puzzle # 204

1	2	7	3	6	4	5	8	9
9	8	3	1	7	5	2	4	6
6	5	4	8	9	2	3	1	7
5	9	2	6	3	8	4	7	1
7	4	8	2	5	1	9	6	3
3	1	6	9	4	7	8	2	5
2	6	5	7	8	3	1	9	4
8	3	9	4	1	6	7	5	2
4	7	1	5	2	9	6	3	8

Harmony Squares: LGBT Sudoku Series

Solution Puzzle # 205

9	6	1	3	7	2	5	8	4
3	7	4	5	1	8	9	6	2
2	5	8	9	4	6	1	3	7
6	8	2	4	3	5	7	9	1
4	3	9	7	8	1	6	2	5
7	1	5	6	2	9	3	4	8
1	9	6	8	5	4	2	7	3
5	4	3	2	9	7	8	1	6
8	2	7	1	6	3	4	5	9

Solution Puzzle # 206

9	3	6	2	7	4	8	1	5
4	2	8	5	6	1	9	3	7
1	7	5	8	9	3	2	6	4
6	1	4	9	8	7	3	5	2
8	9	3	4	2	5	6	7	1
7	5	2	3	1	6	4	9	8
3	4	7	6	5	8	1	2	9
5	6	9	1	4	2	7	8	3
2	8	1	7	3	9	5	4	6

Solution Puzzle # 207

5	4	9	8	2	7	3	1	6
7	2	3	1	9	6	4	8	5
1	8	6	5	4	3	7	2	9
8	5	4	9	6	1	2	3	7
3	1	7	2	5	8	6	9	4
6	9	2	3	7	4	8	5	1
9	7	1	6	8	2	5	4	3
4	3	8	7	1	5	9	6	2
2	6	5	4	3	9	1	7	8

Solution Puzzle # 208

4	2	9	8	5	1	3	7	6
3	6	5	4	7	2	8	9	1
8	7	1	6	3	9	2	4	5
9	1	3	2	4	5	6	8	7
6	5	2	7	1	8	4	3	9
7	8	4	9	6	3	1	5	2
1	9	6	5	8	4	7	2	3
5	4	7	3	2	6	9	1	8
2	3	8	1	9	7	5	6	4

Solution Puzzle # 209

5	3	4	9	7	1	8	6	2
1	7	6	5	2	8	9	3	4
9	8	2	6	4	3	7	5	1
4	5	7	2	8	9	6	1	3
2	1	9	3	6	4	5	8	7
3	6	8	7	1	5	2	4	9
6	9	5	1	3	7	4	2	8
8	2	3	4	9	6	1	7	5
7	4	1	8	5	2	3	9	6

Solution Puzzle # 210

2	6	3	9	7	1	8	4	5
7	9	8	5	4	3	1	2	6
5	4	1	6	2	8	7	9	3
1	2	4	3	5	7	9	6	8
8	7	6	1	9	4	3	5	2
3	5	9	8	6	2	4	7	1
4	1	7	2	3	5	6	8	9
9	3	2	4	8	6	5	1	7
6	8	5	7	1	9	2	3	4

www.ingramcontent.com/pod-product-compliance
Lightning Source LLC
Chambersburg PA
CBHW081005140626
46546CB00019B/3406